GROWTH OF SUGAR COOPERATIVES
AND
ECONOMIC DEVELOPMENT

GROWTH OF SUGAR COOPERATIVES AND ECONOMIC DEVELOPMENT

B.D. Khandare
V.B. Bhise

SERIALS PUBLICATIONS
NEW DELHI

First Published - 2007

ISBN: 81-8387-081-3

Published by

SERIALS PUBLICATIONS
4830/24, Prahlad Street, Ansari Road
Darya Ganj, New Delhi-110002 (India)
Phone : 23245225 Fax : 91-11-23272135
E-mail: serials@satyam.net.in

Contents

	Preface	*vii*
1.	Introduction	1
2.	Review of Literature	24
3.	Policies and Programmes for Development of Sugar Industry in India	47
4.	Growth Trends in Area, Yield, Production and Prices of Sugarcane	77
5.	Growth Trends in Sugarcane Crushed, Sugar Output and Sugar Recovery	100
6.	Impact of Sugar Cooperatives on Economic Development	113
7.	Findings and Policy Measures	136
	Bibliography	147

Preface

The Indian sugar industry is one of the oldest industries in the country. In fact, India is considered as the original home for sugar and sugarcane. About 327 B.C. when Alexander the great invaded India, he and his soldiers were the first Europeans to see sugarcane in India. On their return home, they took sugarcane to Europe. However, it was about 700 A.D. that sugarcane was actually cultivated there. It was between the fourth and sixth centuries that the art of sugar making was discovered in India. The rapid growth of sugar industry in Maharashtra has helped to a very great extent in stabilizing the sugar production in the country and reducing the chronic shortage of sugar. Maharashtra produces about 33 per cent of the total sugar produced in the country and ranks second after U.P. Marathwada, a backward region of Maharashtra state, has good potentials for sugarcane cultivation and development of sugar industry because the land of Marathwada is very fertile and the climate is suitable for growing sugarcane crop. Sugar industry adds to the income of the farmers, provides casual and permanent employment, helps to earn foreign exchange and also helps to develop various kinds of ancillary and by-product industries. This leads to good industrial development and economic development of the region.

This book examines the growth of sugar cooperatives in Marathwada with respect to some parameters such as area, yield and production of sugarcane, sugarcane crushed, sugar recovery, capacity utilization etc. It also assesses the impact of sugar cooperatives on development of this region during the last 23 years. This study makes some important suggestions for the development of sugar industry in this region.

We could make extensive use of library facilities at the Dr. Babasaheb Ambedkar Marathwada University, Aurangabad, Gokhale Institute of Politics and Economics, Pune, Marathwada Agricultural University, Parbhani and Vasantdada Sugar Institute, Manjari (Bk), Pune. We are very much thankful to these institutions. We are also thankful to Shri Babasaheb Akat, Chairman, Marathwada Sarvodaya Shikshan Prasarak Mandal, Partur.

Lastly, we are thankful to Shri Muraleedharan for typing of this manuscript.

B.D. Khandare
V.B. Bhise

1

Introduction

HISTORICAL BACKGROUND

Sugar is known to people of India for more than 2,000 years and there is sufficient evidence to show that India is the original home of cultivating sugarcane and manufacture of sugar. It has been mentioned in the epics as one of the five 'Amrutas'[1]. The sugar industry is the second largest agro-based industry in India next to textile. Though the New Guinea and its neighbouring islands in the South Pacific are now widely believed to be the natural home of sugarcane[2]. The Indian Sugar Industry is one of the oldest industries in the country In fact, India is considered as the original home for sugar and sugarcane. About 327 B.C. when Alexander the great invaded India, he and his soldiers were the first Europeans to see sugarcane in India. On their return home, they took sugarcane to Europe. However, it was about 700 A.D. that sugarcane was actually cultivated there. It was between the fourth and sixth centuries that the art of sugar making was discovered in India.

The Chinese Emperor Tgai-Hang sent a mission to Bihar in about 600 A.D. to study and gather information about the art of sugar manufacture. The knowledge of sugar making was taken from India to Persia. It would thus appear that India had been the original home of sugarcane as also the manufacture of sugar[3].

In the past, India enjoyed monopoly in both production and supply of sugar in the world. Indian sugar used to be exported through the famous caravan routes of Khaiber Pass and Bolan Pass. It used to be shipped to Genoa, Venice and many other countries of Europe and Asia.

Then the first jolt came to the Indian sugar trade in 1453 when the Turks captured Constantinople and demanded heavy royalties on sugar passing through the city. When the British made a successful naval blockade of France, it was a hindrance to France to obtain sugar from India. On Napoleon's order and initiative, France succeeded in the production of sugar out of beetroot. This was followed by bounties which subsidised sugar export from almost all the West European countries and it gave a serious blow to Indian sugar trade and the Indian sugar market was dumped by very cheap sugar from Java and other countries.

The first sugar factory with Vacuum Pan Process and modern milling process was established in Saran district at Marhowrah in Bihar state in the year 1904, while the same was introduced in western world in the year 1853[4].

It is said that less than three hundred years back, in the west, the mass of the people scarcely tasted sugar; it was the rarest of the luxuries and it was even esteemed as a medicine.

But Gangetic India had the knowledge of the sugarcane and the extraction of sugar. Clearly the Chinese acquired the knowledge from India in the first half of the 7th century and finally the Arabs brought the practical art of cultivation of sugarcane to the Western Europe. It was the great age of discovery by the Portuguese and Spaniards carried the sugarcane cultivation over the world. Cane was planted in 1420 A.D. in Madeixa, in 1494 in Santo Domengo. In the early part of sixteenth century, it spread to the West Indies and to the other parts of South America[5].

Cane sugar (sucrose) which is universally used as consumption good spread to other countries evidently from India. Sugarcane growing and making of sugar spread from India to China, Ceylon and Java to Persia in the 6th century and to Spain in the 8th century. The Arabians in the course of their conquest from the 7th to 9th centuries introduced cane growing and sugar manufacture into Cyprus, Egypt, North Africa, Spain and Sicily. Sugarcane cultivation was promoted in all the tropical colonies of the European nations after the discovery of America. It spread to Cuba in 1511, Mexico in 1522, Portorican in 1523, Jamaica in 1527 and in Peru and Brazil at about the same time. In 1751, the Jesuits introduced cane cultivation into Louisiana which afterwards became the chief North American producer of sugar[6].

Sugarcane is a native of Southern Asia obviously first grown in India, during the later period of middle age. Mediterranean countries were also growing the sugarcane. The crop spread rapidly westward from the Mediterranean first to the islands of the American coast and then to the newly discovered American continents, then on cane sugar ceases to be a luxury, instead it became an article of common consumption all over the world[7]. Mr. Minden Wilson had given the historical development of modern sugar in India in his reminiscences of Bihar (1887). In fact, the history of sugar in the remote past is intermingled with the history of indigo and salt peter. In the early part of the 19th century, many indigo and salt peter factories came into existence and slowly they were adopting sugar industry, setting up a few factories along with the indigo industries. After some time, the demand for indigo was declining and when it ceased to be an attraction, the management turned towards sugar industry.

DEVELOPMENT OF SUGAR INDUSTRY IN INDIA

The first sugar factory in India was established in the year 1784 Sooksugar which was privately owned. This factory was started by a cultivator, Croftes. This was followed by starting the second sugar factory in 1791 in Bihar by L.J. Patterson[8].

The then British Government of India introduced the cooperative ideology in 1885 for solving the credit needs of the farmers in this country as per the recommendations of Mr. Nicholson, the officer from Punjab province who was asked to visit the West Germany for studying the problem. Even the British Indian Government realized that the cooperation was the way to solve the problems of the peasants in this country. The first act to promote the cooperative societies and to regulate them was passed in 1904 known as "Co-operative Credit Societies Act 1904" which was amended in 1912. The subject of cooperation was transferred from central list to the concurrent list in 1919 and thereafter the provincial states passed their enactment to promote and regulate cooperative movement in the states. The Bombay Province Co-operative Societies Act was passed in 1925, which laid down 'cooperation as a way of life for better living, better business and better methods of production". Because of all these efforts, the cooperation entered in many economic activities, though with slow pace during pre-independence period.

In 1931 ultimately protection was granted to the sugar industry ushering a glorious chapter in its history. At the time of grant of protection in the year 1932 there were about 31 sugar factories in the whole of India; and the production was about 1.58 lakh tonnes. But in 1939-40, the number of sugar factories has increased to 145 and the production of sugar was amounted to almost more than 3.5 lakh tonnes. In fact, in the year 1936-37, India had attained self-sufficiency in sugar production. The number of sugar factories during the period 1939-40 and 1945-46 remained constant. During the 2nd world war and post-war years, the industry had been in a stagnant condition. Under this prevailing situation, the Government of India appointed the Sugar Commission and Sugar Panel Board. According to their suggestion, India should (1) produce every year 15.5 lakh tonnes of sugar by the year 1950, of which 50.000 tonnes for export, (2) the existing sugar mills should be expanded to at least 800 tonnes per day, and (3) 17 sugar factories should be installed at the cost of crores[9].

After independence, the Government of India laid down the definite approach towards the cooperative movement, in furtherance of their objective of removal of inequalities and the establishment of socialistic pattern of society. The Government of India appointed a committee under the chairmanship of Shri Gorwala in 1951, which is well known as All India Rural Credit Survey Committee. This committee submitted its report in 1954, making far reaching recommendations to revamp the cooperative credit structure in this country. The committee made recommendations to promote the cooperative processing societies of farmers and linking of agricultural credit with agricultural marketing. The committee made the observation and expressed its views that "cooperation has failed but cooperation must succeed". The Government of India has accepted most of the recommendations of the committee and took steps to implement the same. The mind of Government of India to promote cooperative movement and to accept it as a way to bring socialistic pattern of society in this country is reflected in all the plan documents right from the First Five Year Plan.

In the words of the First Five Year Plan Document, "In a regime of planned development, cooperation is an instrument, which while retaining some of the advantages of decentralization and local initiative will yet serve willingly and readily the overall purposes and directions of the plan"[10]. The Second Five Year Plan had stated that "the building up of a cooperative sector as a part of the scheme of planned development is one of the central aims of the national policy. In the area which offer special opportunities for its development, the cooperative form of organization has advantages which neither the system of private enterprise nor that of state ownership can match. In particular, it offers a means of achieving results valuable to the community by drawing equally upon incentives which are social and incentives which are individual[11]. The approach of the government towards the cooperative movement was again reflected in the Third Five Year Plan document in the words,

"In a planned economy pledged to the values of socialism and democracy, cooperation should become progressively the principal basis of organization in many branches of economic life. Cooperation has the merit of "combining freedom and opportunity for the small man with benefits of large scale management and organization as well as goodwill and support from community"[12]. In the subsequent plans too, the Government of India has spelt out in very clear terms, the role assigned to cooperative movement and preferential treatment of the government towards cooperative movement.

This has resulted in entrance of cooperation in many economic activities like agriculture, industry, housing, banking, marketing, distribution, transport, etc. The basic approach laid down by the Government of India after independence towards the cooperative movement, was "the economic development along with democratic lines offers a vast field for the application of cooperation in its infinitive varying forms. Our socialistic pattern of society implies the creation of large number of decentralised units, both in agriculture and in industry. These small units can obtain the advantage of scale and organization mainly by earning together. The character of economic development in India with its emphasis on social change therefore provides a great deal of scope for organization of cooperative activity. The building up of a cooperative sector as part of the scheme of planned development is, thus one of the central aims of national policy.

The view expressed by Prof. D.R. Gadgil, as to why cooperative organization should be encouraged in developing economy would be worth noting in this behalf. He has given two reasons for the same. Firstly, "Planning in the ultimate analysis can be effective only through action of each individual unit of activity in the economy, so that unless the planned target and the pattern of behaviour called forth by plan requirements are communicated effectively to each individual dispersed unit, the success of the plan cannot be guaranteed. Secondly, cooperative organization could be relied not only to implement the plans more effectively, but also to carry them out with greater scrupulousness, care and honesty[13].

The Government of India's policy towards cooperative movement was very much responsible for the development of sugar industry in cooperative sector after independence. According to Ajit Prasad Jain, the then Minister for food and agriculture, Government of India, "the dawn of independence in 1947 brought its wake a change in the outlook and policy of the nation. Our vowed objective is removal of inequalities and early establishment of a socialistic pattern of society. One of the ways for achieving this objective is to encourage peasants to organise and manage processing industries based on the crops produced by them. The establishment of the large number of growers cooperative sugar factories is an effort in that direction"[14]. The Government of India appointed working groups, committees, etc., to make suggestions for development of the cooperative sugar industry through their various policies including licensing, cane price, sugar price and other controls over the sugar industry.

With all their hard and sincere efforts, they succeeded and it was the beginning on large and sound basis of cooperation entering the sugar industry. "The first cooperative sugar factory, which was established at Etikoppaka in Andhra Pradesh though survived, it does not seem to have inspired the development of cooperative sugar factories in India. The credit for initiating this scheme of development of cooperative sugar factories should go to the Pravaranagar co-operative sugar factory established in 1948"[15]

DEVELOPMENT OF SUGAR INDUSTRY IN MAHARASHTRA STATE

It has already been stated that the first factory in Maharashtra was established in 1919 in private sector which was started by the British Company at Haregaon, in Ahmednagar district. The Walchandnagar Industries Limited established their Walchandnagar Sugar Farm in the year 1930 and started its sugar factory. In 1930, the Government of India appointed Tariff Commission to examine the needs of protection to the sugar industry. The commission recommended production protection for a period of 14 years to the sugar industry. Besides, Government of India adopted a favourable policy and provided incentive to the industry[16]. It has resulted in opening of 12 sugar factories in private sector in Maharashtra by the end of Second World War. The private sector sugar factories developed their own sugarcane farms, adopted modern cultivation practices and sown the seeds of sugarcane of improved variety.

No effort was made to organise the cooperative sugar factories in the old Bombay state till 1947 which is a part of the Maharashtra state now. It was only in 1948, the first cooperative sugar factory was established in Ahmednagar district at Pravaranagar. The establishment of cooperative sugar factory at Pravaranagar in 1948 was itself a very good beginning and thereafter many cooperative sugar factories are developed in the state of Maharashtra.

The yield of sugarcane per hectare in the state of Maharashtra is quite high as compared to the yield in the other states except in Tamil Nadu. In 2000-2001, the yield of sugarcane per hectare in the Maharashtra state was of the order of 81.5 tonnes as compared to 54.8 tonnes in Uttar Pradesh and 42.4 tonnes in Bihar, which were otherwise the leaders in the country in respect of sugar industry. It is revealed that the area under sugarcane was 4.60 lakh hectares in the year 1997-98 as against 5.16 lakh hectares during the year 1996-97.

The favourable climatic conditions coupled with adoption of modern methods of cultivation by farmers, hard work by them and development efforts by the sugar factories has resulted in faster growth of sugar industry in Maharashtra. It is however to be taken note of that, results obtained in Maharashtra are not entirely nature's bounty. In the words of Maharashtra Economic Development Council, "The vast smiling green fields of sugarcane which are seen in

Maharashtra today were the success of this co-operative sugar factory created tremendous upsurge amongst the sugarcane growers of the state to organise more and more co-operative sugar factories. The co-operative sugar factories in the state have brought about a change in the crop pattern and through the introduction of better varieties of cane have succeeded in improving substantially the cane yields in their areas and can proudly claim to have obtained the highest recovery among all sugar factories co-operative or joint stock. Alongwith the technological achievements, they have also infused on the atmosphere other powerful social and economic forces, so that the co-operative sugar factories in the state have today came to be regarded as effective spring boards for achieving rural development"[17].

The rapid growth of sugar industry in Maharashtra has helped to a very great extent in stabilising the sugar production in the country and reducing the chronic shortage of sugar. Maharashtra produces about 33 per cent of the total sugar produced in the country and ranks second after U.P.[18]. In 1998-99 there were more than 118 co-operative sugar factories in the co-operative sector and all have been set up at a fairly high block cost compared to the private sugar factories.

It is now an accomplished fact that the soil and climatic conditions of Maharashtra state are favourable for the plantation of sugarcane. The state is located in tropical belt. This belt is famous all over the world as it consists of most suitable areas for raising sugarcane crop. Majority of tho countries producing sugar are situated in this belt. On account of this geographically advantageous position, Maharashtra is renounced as 'sugar bowl' of the country[19].

As regards the aerial spread of the factories, all the private sugar factories are situated only in Western Maharashtra region. The beginning of the co-operative sector has also been in this area only and hence the maximum concentration of factories is found in the Western Maharashtra region. However, of late, the new cooperative sugar factories have entered into the Marathwada and Vidarbha areas. Most important of all the facts that since the agro-climatic conditions in the three regions are different the sugarcane yields as well as recoveries are also different in these areas[20]. Also, "this metamorphosis is neither gift of nature, nor due to fortuitous circumstances. It is a direct result of sustained application of scientific methods to agriculture[21].

DEVELOPMENT OF SUGAR INDUSTRY IN MARATHWADA

The Marathwada region was a part of ex-Hyderabad state under Nizam, till its merger with the old Bombay state in 1948. The first sugar factory was established in 1957 by M/s Dhoot in private sector in Marathwada at Gangapur of Aurangabad district. It was passed on from M/s Dhoot to M/s W.H. Brady and Co., who in turn sold the unit to M/s Belapur Sugar Mills Ltd. This factory was converted into cooperative sector in 1968. This was the beginning of the cooperation entering into sugar industry in Marathwada area. Shri Balasaheb Pawar, the leading cooperator from Aurangabad district provided the leadership for the conversion of Gangapur Sugar Factory into the Gangapur Sahakari Sakhar Karkhana Ltd., in the year 1968. Initially, this factory was taken on lease and license basis by the cooperative society of the farmers and later it became the property of the cooperative society in 1970. Till 1968 as many as 7 licenses were granted to cooperative sugar factories in Marathwada. Since then Marathwada also has made a good headway in the organization of the cooperative sugar factories. The State Government of Maharashtra as a part of its policy to remove imbalance between the developed and the under-developed parts of the state announced special programmes of development for Marathwada region in 1980. In this programme, the assurance was given that efforts will be made to obtain licenses for 5 cooperative sugar factories in Marathwada during the seventh plan period. In pursuance of this announcement made by the state Government, 7 licenses to new cooperative sugar factories were received from the Government of India. The State Government recommended the proposals of new cooperative sugar factories for Marathwada and pursued with the Government of India for grant of licenses to the proposed cooperative sugar factories on priority, Marathwada being a backward region.

In 1985, the Chief Minister of Maharashtra announced new 42 point programme of development for Marathwada which included that efforts will be made to get licenses for additional five sugar factories. These steps of the government have made its own impact on growth of cooperative sugar industry in Marathwada.

By the end of 1985, there were 22 cooperative sugar factories in Marathwada of which 18 were in production and 4 were in the stage of erection. Of these 4 units which were in erection stage during 1985, all are likely to go into production within a years time i.e. by the middle of 1986-87. At present, there are 35 sugar factories in Marathwada region. Marathwada, a backward region of Maharashtra State has good potentials for sugarcane cultivation and development of sugar industry because the land of Marathwada is very fertile and the climate is suitable for growing sugarcane crop. Sugar industry adds to the income of the farmers, provides casual and permanent employment, helps to earn foreign exchange and also helps to develop various kinds of ancillary and by-product industries. This leads to good industrial development and economic development of the region.

IMPORTANCE OF SUGAR INDUSTRY

Sugarcane cultivation is one of the important crops in few states in India. In recent times large proportion of the cane produced is supplied to cater to the needs of sugar industry, whereas in the yester years cane was used for making jaggery. It also supports other industries.

The sugar industry is the second largest agro-based processing industry in India, having certain unique features of its own. It is a seasonal industry, based on a perishable raw material, viz. sugarcane, with by-products like molasses, baggasse etc., which can be utilized:

1. For the production of alcohol and down-stream chemicals.
2. For the fuel requirements of the industry offers the potential to generate additional power supply to the grid. Further baggasse offers tremendous potential to make the country self-sufficient in its requirements of paper and news print.

It has a great significance which cannot be undervalued in its relation to agriculture and industrial economy of the rural regions of India. Fundamentally it affects agriculture. As such the expansion of sugar industry in India is an indispensable point for the upliftment of the socio-economic life of the rural masses, located in the rural areas, it has provided the most effective instrument for carrying progressive trends into the deeper country side.

The most outstanding feature of the sugar industry is the vital link between the factory and the farmers whose interest and well being are interconnected. No other agro-based industry can be compared with sugar industry, in having great impact and close contact between the farmers and factory owners. The cultivation of sugarcane is having a lot of bearing on the teaming unemployment of the country. For example, in the year 1995-96 season, the work force employed by the sugar factories in India which include sizeable number of technical staff and highly trained engineers and chemists is estimated at over 3.5 lakhs. About 25 million cultivators including their dependents are engaged in the cultivation of sugarcane[22].

ROLE OF STATE IN SUGAR COOPERATIVES

The cooperative sugar factories in Maharashtra are an outcome of the partnership among various public authorities, state and central governments, public corporations and the cooperative institutions.

The public corporations that were concerned with the cooperative sugar factories were the Industrial Finance Corporation and the Reserve Bank of India. The cooperative institutions vitally connected with the cooperative sugar factories were the State and District Cooperative Banks and their primary units.

The essence of the scheme of the cooperative sugar factories lay in the democratic and autonomous character of the cooperative institutions.

In fact, the sugar industry is a controlled industry. The Central Government operates various controls over the sugar industry such as fixation of minimum cane prices, regulation of price and movements of sugar and release of sugar quotas for sale. The Central Government also regulates the wages and conditions of service of the clerical, manual and supervisory personnel in the co-operative sugar factories and levies excise income tax on them[23].

The State Government's interest in the co-operative sugar factories was not confined to the contribution to the share capital owned by the factories. It had also intrinsic stake in the successful working of these co-operative sugar factories. As the protector of the public interest the state government was vitally connected with the co-operative sugar factories.

The State Government was intimately interested in the success of these co-operative sugar factories because on it depended the validity of its policy of advancing the co-operative institutions as an alternative to cithor the private sector or the completely government owned public sector. It was vitally connected with the farmers. Its tenancy laws affected the farmers who were the producer members of the co-operative sugar factories. Apart from this the state government possessed the general authority to amend the matters in regard to the co-operative sugar factories.

FINANCIAL PATTERN OF SUGAR CO-OPERATIVES

The terms and conditions of the credits advanced by Industrial Finance Corporation and the Central Financing

Agency took into account the security of their investment, the solvency of the debtor institution and the profit of their operations. They tried to safeguard these by appointing their nominees on the Board of Directors of the co-operative sugar factories. But the ultimate responsibility for safeguarding the security, solvency and profitability of the co-operative sugar factories rested on the shoulders of the nominees of the Board of Directors of these factories[24].

The State Government nominees act on behalf of the Industrial Finance Corporation and the Central Financing Agency in regards to those decisions of the Board of Directors which affected their efficiency and profitability.

The financial participation of the Industrial Finance Corporation, the State Co-operative Bank and the State Government naturally entailed the participation in the management of the co-operative sugar factories by these institutions. The Industrial Finance Corporation advances huge credits to the co-operative sugar factories on the same terms and conditions which were applicable to the private manufacturers. The Industrial Finance Corporation was primarily concerned with the viability and efficiency of the cooperative sugar factories in the same way it was interested in the soundness and profitability of the private manufacturing units[25]

SPECIAL FEATURES OF COOPERATIVE SUGAR MILLS IN MAHARASHTRA

Following are the important features of cooperative sugar mills in Maharashtra:

1. It is only with the cooperative sector coming into operation, because with the encouragement and help of the government, that balanced regional development is taking place. Most of the newly licensed sugar factories are coming up in Vidarbha and Marathwada areas.
2. The co-operative form of organization lent itself as a powerful instrument in the development and

mobilisation of the natural, human and financial resources of the state, in the sugar industry.

3. Another unique feature of the industry in the state is the more meaningful and profitable utilisation of sugarcane compared to all India pattern. During 1995-96, at the all India level only 68.4 per cent of the total cane produced has been utilised by the sugar industry whereas in Maharashtra, 83 per cent of the cane was utilised in the sugar production. Entire credit goes to cooperative sugar factories in Maharashtra[26].
4. As regards the technical performance reference to any journal on sugar would show that the cooperative sugar factories have been continuously attending recoveries of sugar much better than all India average during the last 20 years.
5. The yield of sugarcane in 2000-2001 in Uttar Pradesh and Bihar are 54.8 tonnes and 42.4 tonnes respectively as against 84.4 tonnes in Maharashtra. A sugar recovery of 9.5 per cent if obtained for the whole season is considered satisfactory in U.P. and Bihar while a recovery of 11.5 per cent and above is easily obtained in Maharashtra. A few factories record a recovery of 12.5% and over as an average for a six month season. As a result of high recoveries sugar industry has shifted more and more to the Deccan from its original home in the North. For many years Uttar Pradesh produced 50 per cent of all sugar produced in India, but during the last few years the centre of production has shifted to the south and at present Maharashtra is responsible for providing 33 per cent sugar in their region[27].
6. In addition to the above features, the main feature of the cooperative sector has been its impact and catalytic role in the socio-economic development of the rural areas and in properly harnessing the human resources. Perhaps no industry either in the joint stock or in any other sector in our country has revolutionised the countryside and brought about such a rapid growth in

the economic and social conditions of the rural population to the extent to which the sugar factories have done[28].

GROWTH OF SUGAR INDUSTRY

Organizational

The agroclimatic conditions in Maharashtra are favourable for cane cultivation. The initial experiments demonstrated the profitability of sugarcane cultivation and therefore, wherever there was certainty of annual water supply, increasing demands for organization of sugar factories on cooperative basis came from many corners of the state. This demand sprang from a desire to get a greater share from the value added by processing their own cane. It was felt that these cooperative sugar factories would definitely act as important tools for rural development. The commendable position to the agricultural processing units in cooperative sector was given by the then Prime Minister late Shri Pandit Jawaharlal Nehru and furtherance of this the planning commission assigned priority for organization of sugar factories in the cooperative sector over the units in public and private sector. The share of cooperative sugar factories in total production of sugar is 65 per cent. The Governments both at state and centre took active interest in promotion and establishment of such cooperative units by providing substantial help by way of government share capital, loans, government guarantee to the financing agencies and concessions like waiver of purchase tax, increase in percentage of free sale quota, etc. The earnest efforts of the cane cultivators supported by various incentives from government resulted in rapid growth of cooperative sugar factories in Maharashtra. The table 1 gives a bird's-eye view of the substantial and rapid growth of cooperative sugar industry in Maharashtra in the last five decades.

Table 1
Number of Sugar Factories in Maharashtra

Year	*Cooperative*	*Private*	*Total*
1950-51	1	12	13
1960-61	20	12	32
1970-71	48	11	59
1980-81	71	11	82
1990-91	93	8	101
1995-96	107	4	111
1996-97	112	4	116
1997-98	116	4	120
1998-99	118	4	122
1999-00	119	4	123
2000-01	128	9	137
2001-02	122	13	135
2002-03	145	15	160
2003-04	124	12	136

Source: Performance of sugar factories in Maharashtra, Vasantdada Sugar Institute, Pune, 2003-04.

Growth and Expansion

Initially the sugar factories were established in those areas where assured irrigation facilities were available for supporting cane cultivation. Later, however factories were set up where irrigation sources were from smaller dams and had ample underground water. Agriculturists therefore continued efforts to exploit ground water for cane cultivation[29].

Apart from the organizational growth, due to bringing additional area under cane cultivation and intense efforts for getting increased yield per acre, the sugarcane production has increased to such an extent that the crushing capacity of some cooperative sugar factories needed to be enhanced to cope up with the increased production of sugarcane. Naturally such sugar factories moved in that direction and got the crushing capacity expanded suitably. The following table indicates the present position of range of crushing capacities of sugar factories in Maharashtra state.

Range (TCD)	*Number of factories*
Below 1250	2 cooperative
1250-1500	35
1500-2000	3
2000-2500	8
2500-4900	81
5000 and above	7
	134

Sugar Production

The sugar industry is the second largest industry in India and Maharashtra is the leading sugar manufacturing state in the country. The trend of production of sugar has been increasing except in bad drought years as can be seen from the following table:

Table 2
Growth of Cooperative Sugar Factories and Their Sugar Production in India During 1985-86 to 1998-99.

Particulars	*Unit*	*1985-86*	*1991-92*	*1996-97*	*1998-99*	*2001-02*	*2003-04*
1. Area under sugarcane	'000/ha	265	552	622	630	443	395
2. Yield of sugarcane	Tonnes/ha	89.5	79.83	80.40	90	67.40	59.10
3. Production of sugarcane	000 'tonnes	23706	36187	46616	50850	295956	236176
4. Production of sugar	'000 tonnes	2388	3618	4665	5514	18537	13546

Sources: 1. Cooperative Sugar, December 1998.
2. Krushi Panan Mitra October 2005.

It is expected that this increasing trend would not only be maintained but the speed and rate of increase would have to be improved in order to ensure adequate cane to both existing and the new factories.

SICKNESS OF SUGAR INDUSTRY

In spite of the progress made by the sugar industry in Maharashtra, it cannot be denied that it has to face a number of difficulties. Certain difficulties are such that if they are not solved or if no remedial measures are taken at the appropriate time, they could cause great harm and make a certain portion of the industry permanently sick. The Maharashtra government has been watchful in this respect and has tried to study the problem confronting the sugar industry. They had therefore appointed a committee in the year 1980 under the chairmanship of late Shri Gulabrao Patil, then Chairman of the Maharashtra State Cooperative Bank Ltd., Bombay. This committee studied the causes resulting in the sickness and identified sick cooperative sugar factories and suggested the remedial measures to be taken. The report submitted by this committee in March 1983, was accepted by the government. This committee had identified 19 cooperative sugar factories as sick, and analysed the causes of their sickness. This committee also made certain recommendations to the government[30]

OBJECTIVES OF THE PRESENT STUDY

The following are the main objectives of the present study:

1. To study the policy of the central and state governments towards the sugar industry with particular reference to cooperative sugar factories.
2. To study the trends in area, production and yield of sugarcane in factory areas of Marathwada.
3. To study the trends in sugarcane crushed, production of sugar, capacity utilization, prices paid by cooperative sugar factories and recovery of sugar in Marathwada.
4. To study the impact of sugar cooperatives on employment, agricultural development, education and social life of people in Marathwada.

RESEARCH METHODOLOGY

The present study pertains to Marathwada region and covers the period of 18 years from 1980-81 to 1997-98. At present there are 35 cooperative sugar factories operating in Marathwada. 22 sugar factories were operating in

Marathwada in the year 1980-81. These sugar factories have been considered for the present study. The districtwise distribution of the selected 22 sugar factories in Marathwada is as below:

	District	*No. of Cooperative Sugar Factories*
1.	Aurangabad	5
2.	Jalna	2
3.	Parbhani	3
4.	Beed	4
5.	Nanded	3
6.	Osmanabad	2
7.	Latur	3
	Total	22

Among the seven districts of Marathwada, large number of sugar factories (5) are located in Aurangabad district and very few are located in Osmanabad (2) and Jalna (2) district. All the cooperative sugar factories which are working since 1980-81 are considered for the purpose of the present study.

Now it is important to see the spread over of sugar factories which are in operation in different districts of Marathwada region. There were in all 35 sugar factories in operation during the year 2000-01 in the region. Highest number is registered in Aurangabad followed by three districts viz., Beed, Nanded and Latur consisting 6 sugar factories in each district. Hingoli district is a part of erstwhile Parbhani district. Therefore, only two factories each are shown in operation in Parbhani district in the years 2000 and 2001.

Secondary data about area, production and yield of sugarcane in factory areas, sugarcane crushed, sugar production, sugarcane prices paid by the factories, capacity utilization, sugar recovery, etc. were collected from the annual reports of the sugar factories. Moreover, some data were also collected from the office of the Joint Director of

Sugar, Marathwada region located at Aurangabad, Director of sugar, Government of Maharashtra, Pune, Bharatiya Sugar Directory, Pune and Report of the Maharashtra Rajya Sahakari Karkhana Sangh Ltd., Mumbai. The data about casual employment of cane cutters, permanent employment, educational and other facilities and minor irrigation etc. provided by the cooperative sugar factories were also collected from the office records of sugar factories in Marathwada. In addition to this, some required secondary data were obtained from various periodicals and reports such as Districtwise General Statistical Information of Maharashtra State issued by the Directorate of Agriculture, Godwa (monthly issue), Working Results of Sugar Factories in Maharashtra, Cooperative Sugar , India Sugar, and Handbook of Basic Statistics of Maharashtra State. The data so collected were tabulated and the comparisons are made on the basis of simple growth rates, ratios, averages and percentages.

SCHEME OF CHAPTERS

The present book is divided into seven chapters.

The first chapter deals with the historical background of sugar industry, development of cooperative sugar industry in India, Maharashtra State and Marathwada. It also gives the objectives of the present study, research methodology and scheme of chapters. The second chapter deals with the review of recent and relevant literature appeared on the growth and economic impact of sugar cooperatives in India. The third chapter deals with the review of policies adopted by the Central and State Governments for the development of sugar cooperatives in the country. The fourth chapter deals with the trends in area, production and yield of sugarcane in factory areas of Marathwada. The trends in prices paid by the sugar factories, capacity utilization and working days of sugar factories are also analysed in the same chapter. The fifth chapter deals with the trends in sugarcane crushed, sugar output and sugar recovery of sugar factories located in different districts of Marathwada during the eighties and the nineties. The sixth chapter deals with the impact of sugar cooperatives on employment, agricultural development, educational and other facilities in Marathwada. The welfare and social security scheme implemented by the sugar factories are also discussed in this chapter. The seventh chapter summarises the findings of the present study and their policy implications.

References

1. Indian Sugar Supplement, published by Indian Sugar Mills Association, Sugar House, 39 Nehru Palace, New Delhi, 1948, p. 10.
2. Noel Deer, History of Sugar, Vol. I, Chapman and Hall Ltd., London, 1949, p. 15.
3. Cost Audit in Sugar Industry : The Institute of Cost and Work Accountants of India, Cost Accountant's Hall, 12, Sudder Street, Calcutta, 1971.
4. Prasad J.M., The Indian Nation, April 18, 1976.
5. The World's Sugar Supply : Its Sources and Distribution, National Bank of Commerce, December 1917, pp. 7-8.
6. Gustab Mikusah, Sugar : Encyclopaedia of the Social Sciences, Vol. XIV, The Macmillan Co., New York, pp. 7-9.
7. Minden Wilson: History of Bihar Indigo Factories, Reminiscences of Bihar, The Calcutta General Printing Company, 1908, p. 7.
8. Noel Deer, op. cit., p. 54.
9. N. Ram Vichar Sinha: Sugar Industry in India, Deep and Deep Publications, New Delhi, 1988, p. 20.
10. First Five Year Plan, Government of India, New Delhi, p. 163.
11. Second Five Year Plan Summary, Government of India, p. 83.
12. Third Five Year Plan Summary, Government of India, p. 83.
13. D.R. Gadgil, Towards a Cooperative Commonwealth, Punjab University Publications Bureau, Chandigarh 1961, p. 87.
14. Jain A.P., Foreword to Growers Own Cooperative Sugar Factories, Ministry of Food and Agriculture, Government of India, New Delhi, 1956, p. 10.

15. Inamdar, N.R., Government and Cooperative Sugar Factories, Popular Prakashan, Bombay, 1965, pp. 1-2.
16. Bapat, N.G., Economic Development of Ahmednagar District–1880-1960, Progressive Corporation Pvt. Ltd., Bombay, 1973, p. 312.
17. Shrishrimal, W.C., The Mechanism of Determining Cane Price in Cooperative Sugar Factories in Maharashtra, The Maharashtra Cooperative Quarterly, Vol. L, No. 4, April, 1967, p. 89.
18. Mohite, Y.J., Sugarcane Industry of Maharashtra, (A Blue Print of Progress), Government of Maharashtra, Bombay, 1974, p. 3.
19. Shrishrimal W.C., *op.cit*; pp. 49-52.
20. Mohite Y.J., *op.cit*; p. 47.
21. Agro-Industries in Maharashtra, Problems and Prospects, Maharashtra Economic Development Council Bombay, p. 140.
22. Economic Trends, Vol. XIII, published by Y.L. Sood for FICCI, Federation House, Tansen Marg, New Delhi, September 16, 1985, pp. 5-19.
23. Economic Trends, Vol. XIII, published by Y.L. Sood for FICCI, Federation House, Tansen Marg, New Delhi, June 16, 1984, p. 5.
24. Indian Sugar Year Book, Vol. 1, The Indian Sugar Mills Association, New Delhi, 1983-84, pp. 10-11.
25. Inamdar N.R., Government and Cooperative Sugar Factories, *op. cit.*, pp. 82-83.
26. Ibid, p. 40.
27. Ibid, pp. 33-34.
28. Khanna C.D., 'Sugar Cooperatives : Critical Areas', Cooperative Perspective, Vol. 9, No. 3, October/December, 1974, p. 70.
29. Ibid., p. 71.
30. Ibid, pp. 199-200.

2

Review of Literature

Till 1957, India was importing sugar to meet the consumers needs of the country. Thereafter, sugar industry in India has become one of the important foreign exchange earning industries. The Government of India has taken various measures for its proper growth and development. The government adopted industrial policy which has resulted in setting up of large number of sugar factories in private as well as in cooperative sector. The Industrial Policy Resolution of 1956 has given the preference to setting up of the cooperative sugar factories. Accordingly, right from the First Five Year Plan, emphasis has been given on promoting the cooperative movement, for bringing in the socialistic pattern of society, which is the ultimate objective of the planning in this country. With the advent of growing up of the industry, large number of problems were noticed by the sugar industry itself and by the government in this respect. The problems of the sugar industry were manifold, such as the problem of finance, availability of raw material, problem relating to management, problem relating to the labour and the like. The Government of India appointed various committees from time to time to study the problems of the sugar industry and to make suggestions. Likewise, the state governments also appointed various committees to study the problems of the sugar industry and to make recommendations to the government for taking policy decisions. Besides, various researchers and scholars have made efforts to study the sugar industry from its different angles.

The growth of sugar industry in India has helped the economy in many ways. The cooperative sugar factories have played pivotal role in modernization of agriculture and in the socio-economical and educational transformation of rural society.

It has already been pointed out that the sugar industry being the second largest organised agro-industry in India, plays a vital role in the economy of India, particularly in Maharashtra. It is situated in the rural area owing to the highly perishable nature of the raw material, i.e. sugarcane. The agro-industry leaves a deep impact on the rural economy. With the development in agriculture, it is felt necessary to start and promote related agro-industries, because they not only convert the agricultural goods into finished products but also increase their value.

"The advent of industry makes for the evolution of social structure and way of life and above all, creates and continually reinforces the dynamic resilience of socio-cultural fabric so necessary for material and social progress. In the absence of industrialisation, the forces of change remain weakened. Whatever, if any, betterment of human material agents of development takes place is lost to the regional community through their emigration to industrialized regions. It is, therefore, necessary that along with the agricultural development, industrialisation of the region is initiated and promoted in planned manner"[1].

Taking into account the importance of sugar industry in the national economy a number of researchers have worked on the various aspects of sugar industry such as the development and problems of the sugar industry and its prospects. Similarly, government policy and regional planning for sugar industry area, labour situation of the industry, impact of the industry on the lives of farmers and agriculture, the importance of sugar co-operatives in the rural economy and such other aspects of the industry also have been probed into. In this chapter an attempt is made to review the studies on aforementioned aspects of sugar industry in India after independence.

In 1951, P.M. Devekar studied "The Sugar Industry in Bombay Division"[2]. In this study, he has explained the development of sugar factories and their various problems. He has also discussed the economics of sugarcane and sugar with reference to irrigation, transport, manufacturing etc. Lastly, he explains the prospects of sugar industry in India. He also points out the necessity and importance of sugar co-operatives in the Indian economy.

In 1965, when sugar co-operatives became a significant part of the sugar industry, Inamdar[3] studied the policy of the Government of Maharashtra regarding sugar industry and the potential and practical difficulties in the way of further development of the sugar industry. In this study he considered the necessity of increasing sugar cooperatives in Maharashtra. The efforts of the state government for the development of the industry in the cooperative sector and the help rendered by the institutions like Bombay Provincial Cooperative Bank, Industrial Finance Corporation etc. are discussed therein. Apart from this, the administration of the cooperative sugar factories was also studied.

Kamath[4] has studied the management of cooperative enterprise with special reference to sugar cooperatives in Maharashtra and published his work in 1965. He has studied the problems relating to finance, raw-material, personnel of cooperative sugar factories and managed properly, they can play important role in rural development.

Sirodkar[5] studied the 'Cooperative Movement in Kolhapur District' in 1967. He concluded that the cooperative sugar factories have provided stability to the agricultural income by reasonable and guaranteed price, which has also resulted in increase in sugarcane production. These cooperative sugar factories provide various inputs to the agriculturists. He suggested that the cooperative sugar factories should be established in backward areas so that the backward area can get a chance of its all-round development since the cooperative sugar factories play the role of agencies for rural development. In this work the impact of cooperative sugar factories on agriculture of the Kolhapur district has been analysed by the author. The problems relating to organization, finance, raw material availability have not been dealt with.

Fuss[6] has rightly pointed out that the cooperative sugar factories established in India in larger number have proved to be successful and showed positive effect of extensive Government aid received by them at the time of establishment. Cooperatives have influenced the economic development of farmers. Their success in respective regions have been witnessed by the increased agricultural production, introduction of new agricultural techniques and improved infrastructure and over all change in the rural society.

Bapat[7] studied the economic development of Ahmednagar district for a period of 1880 to 1960. He published his work in 1968. He has given the brief history of development of sugar industry in Ahmednagar district. The role of sugar industry in the development of the rural areas and tho problems of the sugar factories have not been dealt by him.

Hirunandez, Denabay and Corina[8] remarks on the studies relating to sugarcane processing industry are notable. He said that economists have used simple tools i.e. arithmetic average for estimating economies of scale on the basis of empirical data. Such an attempt gives rough estimations about the most optimum capacity size group in respective industry. It is however difficult to conclude exactly as to at what particular point the profit will be maximum. For this, it is necessary to estimate either profit function or cost function from the available data. These functions enable us to determine the optimum capacity as the one having the highest profit or the lowest cost.

Kirilyuk and Kirilyuk[9] have indicated with empirical evidences the need to increase production capacity of the factory from 900-1650 to 1700 tonnes per day in order to achieve economies of scale. Further, they suggested the optimum campaign length of 110 to 115 days.

Roy Choudhary[10] had undertaken a study with a view to observe the problems of the cooperative sugar factories. The results of the study showed that the sugar factories are not only intended for processing sugarcane mainly for sugar but also for a number of by-products. They have no other use, therefore, solely dependent on sugarcane supplied. Sugarcane constitutes the main raw material and forms 70-80 per cent of the cost of production of sugar. The duration of the crushing season has a vital impact upon the economies of the industry. If the crushing season shortens, the cost of sugar production is higher. Exports of the sugar are heavily subsidised, due to the per acre low yield of sugarcane, lower sucrose content, the shorter sugarcane crop season and higher cost of production of sugar.

Aandhale[11] studied the impact of cooperative sugar factory on the lives of the farmers with special reference to Sangamner-bhag Sahakari Sakhar Karkhana Ltd., Sangamner in Ahmednagar district in 1972. He has restricted his work to the impact of sugar factory on the sugarcane producer members of the factory. But it is also clear that non-share holders are equally important in supplying the cane to the factory.

Mohite[12] stated that the rapid growth of sugar industry has been helpful to a great extent in stabilizing sugar production and reducing chronic shortage of sugar in the country. The cooperative form of organization has lent itself as a powerful instrument in the development and mobilization of natural, human and financial resources of the state, towards sugar industry and has helped in reducing the backwardness of the country by improving the socio-economic conditions of rural area in the state.

Malayadri[13] in his work on socio-economic impact of sugar factories has brought out that the sense of consciousness among people at all the levels has been effected due to the cooperative sugar factories. He has considered the impact of cooperative factories on the pattern of sugarcane cultivation. The effect of the sugar factory on irrigation facilities, mobilisation of rural savings, employment in rural area, labour welfare and growth of rural area has also been studied by Malayadri. The reasons of sickness and the poor performance of many of the factories has, however, not been studied.

According to Kamat[14], cooperative sugar factories have not only brought the economics of large scale production to the members but also provided to them with opportunities to organise and manage their own business. The members are trained in democratic and business produces. Though the sugar industry has proved to be one of the great adventures for transformation of Indian economy, it has to face many problems of its own.

According to Kharkar[15] now a days though there is an emphasis on increasing production capacity for the factory, it leads to push the factory in loss due to under utilization of the capacity. The economies of scale are therefore, too obvious to be emphasised in any processing industry. Kharkar has specifically pointed out that economies of sugar factory is disturbed largely because of low productivity and crushing of sugarcane of non-share holders who produce the cane of poor quality. This statement, however, seems to be particularly invalid for the reason that the recovery percentage of sources of sugarcane to factory is quite encouraging.

In 1976, Jain[16] worked on the "Regional Economic Planning in a Sugar Factory Area". Jain had selected the area of Theur Co-operative Sugar Factory of Haveli taluka in Poona district. According to him, the area has not been developed with due consideration of the requirements of the modern technique of regional planning and the needs of the region. Jain has attempted to study the proper demarcation of functions between the sugar factories and other local planning agencies and to determine the propriety of entrusting particular planning functions to an organization like a cooperative sugar factory. Apart from this, he has also considered the problems of sugar industry and reference is made to the important aspects of the impact at the micro level such as impact on irrigation facilities, agricultural development, employment in rural area, etc. But the impact on farmers, industrial and agricultural labours, non-agriculturists, trade and commerce, transport and communication etc are not studied.

Vimala Raghawachari[17] has worked on 'The state and the Indian Sugar Industry'. She has studied the role of the state in the development of sugar industry in India from 1956 to 1970. The study relates to the policy of the state with regard to licensing and location of the sugar factories, financing the sugar industry and controls of the state on sugar industry. The prospects of the sugar industry have been discussed by the author. The importance of cooperative sugar factories has also been studied.

Mittal[18] has given some of the suggestions for improving economics of sugar industry as follows:

1. Adoption of techniques to reduce losses of sugar,
2. Utilization of by-products,
3. Increasing productivity of sugarcane,
4. Reduction in store consumption,
5. Changing formula of levy prices fixation, and
6. Payment to cane growers according to cane quality rather than weight.

The Report of the Programme on Cost Accounting and Financial Management (1976) indicated that, because of increase in the capital investment in the new units, the loan requirement increased to a greater extent and this has resulted into high interest cost and high depreciation which prohibited the sugar units to make any profit.

According to Thaper[19], some of the peculiar features of the sugar industry are as follows :

(a) The industry is seasonal.

(b) Duration of season varies from one factory to other and also from year to year.

(c) Sugar content in cane and its recoveries also vary at random from one factory to another.

(d) Variation in capital investment.

Apart from the problem of cyclical nature of production of sugar and variation in capital investment and sugar recovery, the sugar industry experiences inter-state differences in the cost of production per unit of sugar. The cost of production of sugar as estimated by Pothuwal (1972) in Uttar Pradesh and Dhanuka (1975) in Bihar varied between Rs. 107.05 and Rs. 270.0 per quintal, the biggest and the lowest being in Uttar Pradesh and Bihar respectively.

Ferron[20] has rightly said that there is a necessity of determining the most economic size of sugar mill in order to safeguard the industry from the problem of diseconomies. The basic consideration in determining the milling capacity of sugarcane mill must therefore, be illustrated as the basis of production cost and performance figures of factory.

Mohite[21] has said that the rapid growth of sugar industry has been helpful to a great extent in stabilizing sugar production and in reducing chronic shortage of sugar in the country. The cooperative form of organization has lent itself as a powerful instrument in the development and mobilization of natural, human and financial resources of the state towards sugar industry and has helped in reducing the backwardness of the country by improving the socio-economic conditions of rural areas in the state.

Gadgil[22], an eminent economist, who was also the promoter of the first cooperative sugar factory in India, has made lot of contribution to the literature on the cooperative sugar factories. In his study on 'Sugar Cooperatives in Maharashtra' he has dealt with the growth and prospects of the sugar industry in Maharashtra. The reasons of the rapid growth of sugar industry in Maharashtra have been highlighted. He has written number of articles on the role of sugar industry on the rural development touching to the various problems of the sugar industry.

Pawar[23] while studying economies of scale in cooperative sugar units in Maharashtra, concluded that per unit profitability of sugar production was low in large sized factories as compared to smaller ones in 1977. Large sized factories, however were at advantages in economising manufacturing expenses and overhead costs provided the cane price and excise duty remained the same for all factories. Further, he stated that the large sized factories could derive economies of scale by utilizing their capacities to a higher level. These factories were in loss due to insufficient supply of cane. According to him, the problem of insufficient supply of cane could be solved by increasing area under cane as well as by increasing productivity of cane. Limitations on irrigation supply, however brings about restraint on expansion of area under cane cultivation. The only alternative left is, therefore, to increase sugarcane yield per unit of area.

Patil[24] has attempted to examine the correlation among sugarcane area, average yield per hectare and sugar recovery in Maharashtra. The data were collected from 1950-61 to 1975-76 and the correlation among sugarcane area, average yield and sugar recovery was examined using the technique of correlation and regression analysis. The study for regression equation was proceeded for the components significantly correlated and expected sugar recovery percentage was cultivated by using regression equation. The result revealed that there was a significant negative correlation [r = (-) 0.4375] between area and sugar recovery per cent while correlation among sugarcane area and yield, sugarcane yield and sugar recovery were nonsignificant. Negative and significant correlation between sugarcane area and sugar recovery at 5 per cent level indicated that increased sugarcane area, deteriorated the sugar recovery.

Kawade[25] determined optimum use level of production capacity of the cooperative sugar factories in Maharashtra on the basis of the behaviour of operating and total costs relative to installed capacity of the sugar factories. Two cost functions have been estimated on the basis of the data on average total cost (ATC) per quintal of sugar and average variable cost (AVC) per quintal of sugar in relation to installed capacity of the sugar factories (T). Average total cost and average variable cost were regressed separately on the installed capacity and the following empirical relation of the quadratic type were obtained.

$$(1)\ ATC = 246.24 - 0.010053\ T + 0.000003467\ T^2$$
$$(0.003052) \quad (0.0000066)$$

$$(2)\ AVC = 226.02 - 0.01044\ T + 0.000003523\ T^2$$
$$(0.002337) \quad 0.0000006114$$

$$R^2 = 0.8406.$$

The minimum cost point appeared at 1455 tonnes and 1482 tonnes of installed capacity per day respectively, for the ATC and AVC cost curves. From this analysis, it appears that both ATC and AVC firstly decreased and then increased with the installed capacity.

Kharche[26] studied the cane development programme in sugar factory area with special reference to sick factories and found that the low production of sugarcane in factory area was due to:

1. Inadequate staff for implementation of sugarcane development scheme,
2. Lack of arrangements for hot water treatment and the mercuric compound treatment to the seed,
3. Untimely availability of finances,
4. Primitive method of cultivation of sugarcane, and

5. Inability of the sick units to pay even the minimum cane price.

All these factors together limit the supply of cane to the factories, which results in very poor crushing and still more losses.

Raghwendra[27] stated that the problems of sugar industry (factory) emerge right from the starting of crushing season and they continue right up to the deciding of the price of sugarcane, payment of workers, distribution of sugar, etc.

Singh and Swarup[28] have shown that sugarcane production in the country was found to have increased at the compound rate of 0.80 per cent per annum. In the First Five Year Plan the compound growth rates of production increased to 6.6 per cent and 6.80 per cent per annum in the second and third Five Year Plan respectively. During the Fourth Plan the rate of increase came down to 0.70 per cent per annum. During First Five Year Plan, higher growth rate in production was observed in Tamil Nadu and Karnataka, while in Second Five Year Plan, this position was shared by Maharashtra State, Punjab, Tamil Nadu and Karnataka. In the Fourth Five Year Plan, it was in Tamil Nadu only that a higher growth rate was shown.

Anon[29] reported that Eid-Parry Ltd. sugar factory in Tamil Nadu incurred loss of Rs. 4.11 crores due to the lower working efficiency and less crushing days in a season. The factory could not be run efficiently due to mechanical defects and labour problems. The start of the sugar factory was delayed due to several adverse factors affecting the number of working days.

Pawar and Kshirsagar[30] studied the trends and variability of area, production and productivity of sugarcane in Maharashtra and Uttar Pradesh. This study indicated that though the area and production of sugarcane in both the states increased over a period of 25 years, there were wide fluctuations in area and production of sugarcane on yearly basis which affected the supplies of cane to the sugar industry directly. The study, therefore, maintained that for stabilization of the sugar production, it is necessary to stabilize acreage under sugarcane through appropriate manipulation of price and non-price factors.

In April 1980, Government of Maharashtra appointed a Committee[31] under the Chairmanship of Shri V.P. Rane, the Director of Sugar, Maharashtra State, for making recommendations for the formation of zones for sugar factories. The committee submitted its report in 1983. The Committee observed that as per the sugarcane control order of 1966, there were overlapping villages allotted among the nearest sugar factories, because of which steps for sugarcane development could not be taken by the concerned sugar factories. In the same way crisscross movement of sugarcane resulted in increasing cost of transport and ultimately in cost of production of sugar. The Committee has discussed the factors determining viability of a sugar factory and recommended that a factory should be permitted to have capacity of at least 2000 TCD, and for achieving economies of scale there should be no upper limit on the crushing capacity. The Committee lastly recommended zones for every sugar factory in Maharashtra.

Ramesh[32] stated that the sugar industry in India is the second largest processing industry in the country next only to textile. There are 320 factories producing annually 6570 lakh tonnes of sugar. The aggregate assets of the industry are more than Rs. 1300 crores. About 30 million cultivators are engaged in growing sugarcane and supplying the same to sugar factories. The sugar industry disburses about Rs. 800 crores annually towards the sugarcane price. It contributes more than Rs. 300 crores annually to state and central exchequers. The factories are ideally suited for faster rural socio-economic development. The prosperity of the sugar industry is, therefore, closely linked with the development and prosperity of our vast population residing in the villages.

Shah and Shah[33] pointed out that the cost of production of sugar factory depends primary on the raw materials, the sugar recovery percentage and the duration of crushing season. They suggested that the cost of sugar production can be brought down by utilizing the processing unit for a maximum period, the proper checking of the machinery of its day to day work, the cost of extra fuel, lubricants, spare parts, consumption of chemicals, and sugar content in final molasses would be reduced, if the steam balance and machinery maintained, proper plans and proper watch in clarification and boiling house stations.

Murali[34] suggested that break-even analysis is an important aspect for proper planning of sugar industry and controlling its profits. It helps in determining:

1. Minimum level of operation required to avoid losses,
2. Volume of sale to be undertaken to achieve a profit target,
3. The effect of change in price, change in fixed costs, change in variable cost and change in volume of sales on profit and
4. Assessment of the proportion and sales mix to maximize profits.

Manohar Rao[35] rightly pointed out that the current international prices of sugar and molasses, every sugar producing country has a strong reason to convert sugarcane into sugar and molasses to earn foreign exchange required for keeping up the balance of trade. It may be even economical to import crude out of the foreign exchange earned by export of sugar and molasses. However, as the international price of sugar is fluctuating widely and for reducing the dependence on other countries for import of crude gradually for political reasons, the sugar producing countries may have to convert the molasses into alcohol and also consider the possibilities of converting a part of the sugar juice into alcohol. He further concluded that it was more economical to convert sugarcane into sugar and molasses and to use molasses as raw material for production of ethyl alcohol. The economics of these activities will however, largely depend on the international price of sugar, molasses and ethyl alcohol.

Ingram[36] studied the economies of production of alcohol from molasses and sugarcane. The study indicated that the investment and operation costs depend on the distillery system used (centralized integrated or autonomous distilleries) and the costs are recalculated for an autonomous plant. Comparison was made between the prices of gasoline and a 85:15 blend and also relationship between ethanol price and cane price was worked out. The study emphasized that the world price of sugar directly affects the price of cane and that a high price of sugar would probably significantly reduce the availability of sugarcane fort a sucro-chemical industry.

Singh[37] reported that the byproducts of sugar factories were neglected continuously and income from by-product was lost. The realization from the by-product of sugar factory represents about 1 to 3 per cent of the value of sugar. He suggested that if the by-product of sugar factories (i.e. bagasses, molasses, filter mud, boiler ashes and sugarcane tops) were put to right use, they could generate new hope for the sick sugar mills and job opportunities for thousands of the employees. The sugar technologists have pointed out that if all the by-products are utilized in a sugar factory, its probability may increase by as much as 50 per cent depending on the products which it chooses to adopt from the by-products.

Tupe[38] in his work on 'Impact of Sugar Factories on the Rural Economy–A Case Study' has studied in detail the impact of Sanjivani Cooperative Sugar Factory in Ahmednagar district on agriculture, agriculturists, on the lives of agriculture labour, economic conditions of factory workers and spread effects of the sugar factory and overall economic change in rural area. He concluded with the findings that sugarcane being the cash crop, area under sugarcane has increased, the area under irrigation has increased and likewise the change in the cropping pattern and methods of farming have changed. It is argued that the development of agriculture depends on major agro-based industries. The real income of the farmers has increased but the real income of the agricultural labourers has been decreased. It is concluded by the author that sugar factory in rural area has worked as a growth centre.

The Government of Maharashtra[39] appointed a Committee for studying the problem of sick cooperative sugar factories under the chairmanship of Shri Gulabrao Patil. The Committee found that inadequate supply of sugarcane, lack of sugarcane, substantial increase in the project cost and lack of term loan arrangements, associated with relatively lower owner equity and excess burden of interest on short term loans, lack of experienced technical personnel for efficient use of machinery, inefficient management and lack of long term price policy for sugarcane, were the major reasons for sustained losses from sugar production on a continual basis.

Sharma[40] has stated that co-operative sugar factories help farmers for getting more yield by following ways:

1. Distribution of good quality cane which is disease free and improved varieties for planting.
2. Land preparation to provide agricultural implements.
3. Irrigation facilities.
4. Technical knowledge of crop rotation, inter cropping by different trials and demonstration.

Rao[41] has pointed out that the factors like inability of sugar factory to operate at the rated capacity during the seasons, over capitalization in cooperative sugar factories and quality of the management were the most important reasons for the sugar factories in Maharashtra to become sick.

Kohak[42] has studied the socio-economic effects of a cooperative sugar factory on agriculture, cultivators and on agricultural labourers. He had chosen the Niphad Shetkari Sahakari Sakhar Karkhana in Nasik district. He also studied the impact of sugar factory on the development of infrastructure, social services like education, medical facilities, capital formation, employment generation in the area of operation of sugar factory. From this study, he concluded that because of the establishment of the sugar factory, the tendency of depending solely on the cash crop like sugarcane has been increasing among the farmers, which may ultimately have adverse effect on other farmers. Secondly, sugarcane requires proportionately more water compared to other crops i.e. nearly for a period between 15 and 18 months till its maturity. If the available water is used for other crops of 3 to 4 months duration, more land can be brought under irrigation. This will help in increasing agricultural productivity and it is the need of the time. He also concludes that a cooperative sugar factory accelerates economic development in its area of operation only.

Hapse[43] reported that the factors like inadequate supply of sugarcane due to lack of sugarcane development programme, lack of irrigation facilities, lack of regulation in sugarcane supply due to inadequate control leading to cane scramble, inadequate own funds, excess burden of interest on temporary or short loan, unrealistic sugar and sugarcane prices, lack of efficient management, lack of expertise in the board of directors, competitions of gur and khandsari units and lack of long-term sugar policy are the root causes for the sickness of the cooperative sugar factories in Maharashtra.

Jagdish Lal and Bajpai[44] have indicated that growth rate of sugarcane production was highest in Tamil Nadu followed by Karnataka, Maharashtra, Punjab, Uttar Pradesh, Andhra Pradesh and Bihar. Most of the tropical states had growth rates of area, production and prices, higher than those of sub-tropical states. The states having high growth rates of cane or gur, prices also had higher growth rates of area and or production. In the states with higher growth rates of area and or production, the variability in area, production, productivity and price were observed to be higher in the states having higher growth rates of these variables. They have said that it is desirable to bring about substantial improvement in productivity for which efforts should be made for replacement of currently grown varieties with superior ones, timely and adequate supply of strategic inputs, effective transfer of plant and ratoon sugarcane technology, control of disease and pests, drainage for water logged areas, reclamation of saline alkali soils and timely payment of cane price to farmers.

The major causes of sickness of sugar mills were identified by the Reserve Bank of India Group[45]. They are as follows :

1. Shortage of raw material-sugarcane,
2. Lack of cohesion between the price of sugarcane, cost of production and sugar sale realisation,
3. Unplanned growth of units,
4. Under utilization of capacity,
5. Deficiency of plant and machinery and
6. Excessive labour force.

Remedial measures suggested by the group are the following :

1. Increasing the area and yield per acre of sugarcane.
2. Expansion of capacity of uneconomic units to 2000 TCD.
3. Reduction of excessive labour strength by granting retrenchment benefits.
4. Provision of soft loan.
5. Remission of basic excise duty.
6. Grant of higher incremental levy price of Rs. 45/- per quintal.
7. Grant of extra free sales quota.
8. Waiving of principal loan amount.

Kharche[46] has worked on the topic "Cooperative Sugar Factories in Marathwada-A critical study" for his Ph.D. degree examination in 1987. In his work, he has discussed the licensing policy of sugar industry of the Government of India. Further, he analysed financial structure of cooperative sugar factories. In connection with the efficiency of sugar factories, the importance of the supply of sugarcane,

sugarcane development activities and other problems relating to the supply of raw material i.e. sugarcane, are also discussed in this thesis. Furthermore, he has also studied the cost of production of sugar, role of management in the development of the sugar factories and the spread effects of cooperative sugar factories in their areas of operation. Finally, he has analysed the causes of sickness of sugar factories and has made some recommendations to overcome the problems of sickness.

Kuchhadiya, Shiyani and Parmar[47] observed an increasing trend in all the variables of sugarcane and sugar production in Gujarat and India as a whole, however the growth rates were comparatively higher in the state as compared to the country as a whole. Furthermore, they revealed that the variability of production was more than the variability in area and yield of sugarcane in Gujarat as well as in India and arrived at the conclusion that the cultivation of sugarcane crop in the Gujarat state was profitable to the farmers.

The study of Hinge, Pawar and Narwadkar[48] showed that the installed capacity was over utilized in the healthy class while in the remaining classes, it was under utilized due to inadequate cane supply which in turn influenced per unit cost of production. The gap between the highest and the lowest per quintal cost of manufacturing sugar was Rs. 118.3. The per sugar factory per annum value of sugar was the highest in the healthy class followed by medium and sick sugar factories. The sugar factories belonging to all the classes incurred loss. However, the loss was the highest in case of the sick sugar factories. The net loss of 100 tonnes of installed capacity was observed to be largely influenced by the magnitude of return from sugar production. In spite of the low per unit cost of production of sugar, the overhead costs, were relatively very high in the case of sick sugar factories. These sugar factories sustained heavy losses. The economies of scale entirely depend on the ability of sugar factories to fully utilize the installed capacity.

Kasar and Tilekar's study[49] indicated that the sugar industry has significant impact on the employment of seasonal migrants in Maharashtra. The share of sugar factory employment was to the extent of 45.51 and 75 per cent in the total employment of an average male, female and bullock pair of the migrant household. As regards the income, it is noted that the sugar industry, on an average contributes 57 per cent of the gross income of migrant household. The seasonal employment provided by the sugar industry enabled the migrant households to increase their income to enjoy a slightly better position as compared to the non-migrants under study. Therefore, the policy has been endorsed for the installation of agro-processing industries based on local raw produce in rural areas in order to generate employment and income opportunities for the economic development of weaker sections.

Singh, Malik and Lal[50] have examined the growth trends and variability in acreage, production and productivity of sugarcane in Uttar Pradesh for the period 1970-71 to 1990-91. Exponential equation i.e. $y = ab^t$ was used to work out the annual compound growth rates of area, production and productivity of sugarcane. They concluded that the acreage, production and productivity of sugarcane have increased with moderate year to year, fluctuation in different agro-economic regions and Uttar Pradesh as a whole except Bundel Khand region of the state. The major fluctuation trends were seen in area, production and productivity of sugarcane in all the regions while that of minor fluctuation trends in western region. The major factors significantly and positively affecting sugarcane acreage were rainfall, gur price, competitive crop price and current years price of sugarcane. Further, it was also noted that rainfall during the months of July, August and September, flow of canal water and proper supply of electricity during the hot month period, inadequate knowledge about the sugarcane production in the state were the important factors. Other factors like timely availability of input factors, poor management of agro-economic practices, lack of high-yielding varieties were also responsible for low productivity of sugarcane in the state.

Thus, various scholars have studied the different aspects of the sugar industry separately. It should be emphasized here that whenever a particular factory is established in a region, it influences the economy of the region in all its aspects from all the angles. Hence, it would be better to take into consideration the impact of a factory as a whole and not by parts. In the present study, in addition to these aspects already mentioned, attempt has been made to study the growth of sugar cooperatives, its impact of economic development as a whole as influenced by the sugar factory in its area of operation. A very few studies have been conducted so far on the growth of sugar cooperatives at the Marathwada region level.

References

1. Brahme S., Pore K. and Pore S.H., Regional Planning : A Case Study of Marathwada Region, Gokhale Institute of Politics and Economics, Poona, 1975, p. 30.
2. Devekar P.M., Sugar Industry in Bombay Division, M.Com. Thesis, University of Bombay, 1951.
3. Inamdar N.R., Government and Cooperative Sugar Factories, Popular Prakashan, Bombay, 1965.
4. Kamath G.S., Management of a Cooperative Enterprise with Special Reference to Sugar Cooperatives in Maharashtra, Ph.D. Thesis, Poona University, 1965.
5. Shirodkar S.L., Cooperative Movement in Kolhapur District, Ph.D. Thesis, University of Poona, 1967.
6. Fuss F.W., Cooperative Factories in India, World Agricultural Economics and Rural Sociology, Abstract, 1968, p. 75.
7. Bapat N.G., Economic Development of Ahmednagar District, 1881-1960, Bombay Progressive Corporation, 1973.
8. Hirunandas J., Denabox F. and Corina M., Study on Economies of Scale in Raw Sugar Factories, The International Sugar Journal, July, 1971, p. 211.
9. Kirilyak A.P. and Kirilyak L.A., The Production Capacity of Sugar Factory and Optimum Campaign Length, International Sugar Journal, February, 1971, p. 56.

10. Roy Choudhary, Problems of the Cooperative Sugar Factories, Indian Cooperative Review, 1972, p. 65.
11. Andhale G.B.., A Study of the Impact of a Cooperative Sugar Factory on the Lives of Farmers, M.Sc. (Agri.) Thesis, Mahatma Phule Krishi Vidyapeeth, Rahuri, 1972.
12. Mohite V.J., Productivity of Sugarcane Changing Pattern, Sugarcane Industry of Maharashtra, A Blue Print for Progress, Government of Maharashtra, 1974, p. 18.
13. Malyadriv, Socio-Economic Impact of Sugar Cooperatives, Commerce Publication, 1975.
14. Kamat G.S., Management of Cooperative Sugar Factories in Maharashtra, The Maharashtra Cooperative Quarterly, LIX(3), 1975, p. 175.
15. Kharkar N.C., Technological Evaluation of Sugar Factories in Maharashtra, Deccan Sugar Technologists Association, Pune, 1975, p. 15.
16. Jain N.S., Regional Economic Planning in a Sugar Factory Area, Ph.D. Thesis, University of Poona, 1976.
17. Raghavachari V. , State and the Indian Sugar Industry, Ph.D. Thesis, University of Poona, 1973.
18. Mittal B.L., Rehabilitation and Modernization of Sugar Factories, Sugar Technology, Indian Sugar, 26(5), 1976, p. 281.
19. Thapar B.M., Way in Sugar Industry Sick, Financial Express, December 1976.
20. Ferron, Oliva D.P., Sugar Industry in Bihar Diagnosis and Remedy, Indian Sugar, 26(6), 1976, p. 433.
21. Mohite V.J., op. cit.
22. Gadgil D.R., Sugar Cooperatives in Maharashtra, Published by the National Federation of Cooperative Sugar Factories Ltd., New Delhi, 1961.
23. Pawar J.R., Cooperative Sugar Units in Maharashtra: Economies of Scale, The Economic Times, 16(330), 1977, p. 5.
24. Patil M.K., Rehabilitation and Modernization of Cooperative Sugar Industry, Maharashtra Sugar, 2(1), 1976, p. 120.
25. Kawade A.V., Economies of Size and Returns to Scale in Cooperative Sugar Factories in Maharashtra, M.Sc. (Agri.) Thesis, Mahatma Phule Agricultural University, Rahuri, 1977.

26. Kharche R.M., A Cooperative Sugar Industry in Marathwada, Lead Industry for Development, Reference to Sick Factories from Marathwada and Vidarbha, 2(5), 1977, p. 15.
27. Raghwendra P.G., Sugar Factories and Their Problems, Maharashtra Sugar, 1(7), 1977, p. 67.
28. Singh Rajendra and Swaroop, Regional Differences in Sugarcane Output Growth in India, Indian Sugar, 28(4), 1978, p. 189.
29. Anon, Company Affairs, Eid-Parry (India) Ltd., Indian Sugar, 24(2), 1979, p. 195.
30. Pawar G.R. and Kshirsagar S.M., Growth Rate in Area, Production and Productivity of Sugarcane in Comparison with Important Cash Crops in Maharashtra, Maharashtra Sugar, 4(11), 1979, p. 14.
31. Gadgil D.R., op. cit.
32. Ramesh N.A., Adjudication of the Performance of Sugar Factories, Maharashtra Sugar 6(4), 1980, p. 47.
33. Shah H.P. and Shah N.K., Measures for Reduction in Cost of Production of Sugar, Gujarat Association for Agricultural Science, 1980.
34. Murali P., Sugar Industry Planning and Controlling Profiles, Maharashtra Sugar, 5(5), 1980, p. 39.
35. Manohar Rao P.J., By-Products Utilization in Sugar Industry, Maharashtra Sugar, 6(5), 1980, p. 36.
36. Ingram L., Fuel and Chemical Feed Stock from Sugarcane in Central America, International Sugar, 82, 1980, p. 319.
37. Singh R.V., Wealth from Sugarcane Waste, Yojana, 24 (9), 1980, p. 7.
38. Tupe S.D., The Impact of Sugar Factories on the Rural Economy – A Case Study, Ph.D. Thesis, University of Poona, 1980.
39. Government of Maharashtra, Sugarcane Control Order, dated 28th March, 1985, p. 3.
40. Sharma S.C., The Role of Sugar Industry in Rural Development with Special Reference to East Uttar Pradesh., North Bihar, Indian Sugar, 31(6), 1981, p. 395.
41. Rao Birendra Singh, Licensing for New Sugar Factories to be Reviewed, Agricultural Situation in India, 4(4), 1985, p. 277.

42. Deshmukh Datta, Maharashtratil Sakhar Kampanya, Mothya Usmalyavaril Kamgar va Khomdkari, Zamin Malakanche Prashna, Published by Datta Deshmukh, Sangamner, 1983, p. 22.
43. Hapse D.G., Sugar Development Technology for Maharashtra, Maharashtra Sugar, 8(2), 1982, p. 51.
44. Jagdish Lal and R.K. Bajpai, Measuring Growth in Area, Production, Productivity and Prices of Sugarcane and its Competing Crops and Gur in India, Bharatiya Sugar, 11(9), 1986, p. 71.
45. Onnen T.T. and Choda Rajkumar, Management Effectiveness for Revival of Sick Sugar Factories, Bharatiya Sugar, 12(4), 1987, p. 15.
46. Government of Maharashtra, Sugarcane Control Order, Published by Government of Maharashtra, 1966, p. 4.
47. Kuchhadiya D.B., Shiyani B.L. and Parmar G.D., An Economic Analysis of Sugarcane Crop, Indian Sugar, 39(9), 1988, p. 739.
48. Hinge V.N., Pawar J.R. and Narwadkar D.S., Production Performance of Cooperative Sugar Units in Maharashtra, Indian Journal of Agricultural Economics, XIV(3), 1989, p. 343.
49. Kasar D.V. and Tilekar S.N., Impact of Sugar Industry on Employment and Income of Seasonal Migratory from Households in Maharashtra, Indian Journal of Agricultural Economics, Vol. 44, No. 3, 1989, p. 329.
50. Singh K.V., Malik, Sanjeev Kumar and Lal Jagdish, Inter-regional Trend Analysis of Sugarcane Acreage, Production and Productivity in Uttar Pradesh, Agricultural Situation in India, Vol. XLIX, No. 3, May, 1994.

3

Policies and Programmes for Development of Sugar Industry in India

The government policy regulates almost every aspect of sugar industry such as regulation and pricing of sugarcane, quality, storage and release of sugar stocks; control over price and distribution of by-products like molasses and alcohol, regulation of wages etc. Similarly, financing of sugar industry, be it for financing of new projects or credit facilities for other purposes like purchase of cane, stock of sugar etc. is severely controlled by the financial institutions and banks under overall directions from Governmont of India or Reserve Bank of India. Even with regard to the sale of free quota sugar, its release, trading and stocking by the traders, the regulations are so severe that not much is left for the market speculation.

The main policy pillars which govern the functioning of the sugar industry include licensing policy, financing policy, pricing policy, schemes for development of sugar industry, etc. An attempt is made in this chapter to take a brief review of these policies framed by the government for the development of sugar industry in the country.

LICENSING POLICY

There has been continuous expansion of production capacity in the sugar industry. In 1997, there were 412 installed sugar factories with 2,70,975 thousand metric tonnes sugar production[1]. Licensing of the sugar factories was decided by the Central Government. So, let us take a look at the Central Government Licensing Policy.

Sugar industry was governed by provincial governments till 1952. Government passed the Industries (Development and Regulations) Act 1951, which controlled the grant of licenses to sugar industries by appointing adhoc-licensing committees. The first adhoc committee was appointed in 1954.

First Licensing Committee

The committee decided on following criteria for the grant of licenses[2].

1. Availability of sugarcane and facilities for transporting raw material to sugar factories.
2. The possibility of developing sugarcane cultivation in the area.
3. Technical feasibility and economic viability of the proposed project.
4. Capacity of the entrepreneur to complete the proposed project in time.

These criteria ensure that when a new sugar factory is established, it should be able to utilize the capacity fully with proper supply of cane and raw material and with passage of time, should also be able to expand the existing capacity with further development of sugarcane cultivation in surrounding area and make the unit profitable.

Second Licensing Committee

In 1954, there were 134 sugar factories in operation. Afterwards, new licenses were issued as per the above recommendations of the First Licensing Committee. In 10 years time i.e. (1964), 58 new units were established. In 1964, there were 192 sugar factories in operation. In 1964, the government appointed Second Licensing Committee. In addition to the recommendations of the first committee, second committee recommended following criteria[3] :

1. First priority should be given to expansion of existing and uneconomic units.
2. Second priority should be given to the new units in co-operative sector. They recommended the crushing capacity daily between 1200 tonnes and 2000 tonnes.
3. The units which could develop by-products through expansion should be given preference.

As mentioned earlier, the targets of licensing of sugar factories depend upon a number of factors like requirement of sugar for internal consumption, exports and buffer stocks. These requirements decide as to how many new licenses and how many licenses for expansion are to be given.

Along with all these aspects of licensing, it must be emphasized that government has maintained a preferential licensing policy towards the co-operative sector.

Licensing Guidelines and Five Year Plans

In addition to the Central Government's licensing policy, the five year plans also set the guidelines for the growth of sugar industry. The five year plans acknowledged the importance of co-operative sector in the growth of sugar industry and this was reflected in the guidelines for issue of licenses. We shall take a brief review of the sixth and seventh plan licensing guidelines.

Sixth Plan Guidelines

Sixth plan recommended the following criteria for issue of licenses:

1. Preferential treatment to the co-operative sector should continue.

2. New sugar factory can be established in an area where there is abundant sugarcane already or there is good potential for sugarcane development around the site of the proposed factory.
3. To ensure adequate supply of cane to existing units as well as future expansion, no license should normally be granted for new factory within a distance of 30 km of existing factory.
4. Where there are large number of sugar factories located in one district, State Government should make proper zoning of sugarcane areas for each existing factory before considering new licenses of expansion of existing units[4].

The Government of India revised the above policy and through a press note laid down two more criteria for licensing. These new additional guidelines were applicable up to the end of sixth plan period. The new guidelines were as follows[5]:

1. Expansion of existing units will normally not be permitted beyond 3500 TCD. Expansion of capacity beyond 3500 TCD would be permitted only in exceptional cases and purely on merit and technical considerations, with a view to establish agro-industrial complex.
2. Subject to economic feasibility, licensing of new sugar factories might be confined to districts where sufficient cane is grown at present, but where no sugar factories are existing or have been licensed.

Based on these guidelines, by the end of 6th plan, 57 licenses for new sugar factories and 48 licenses for expansion of existing factories were given. Out of these, 18 new factories and 27 expansion licenses were granted in the state of Maharashtra.

Seventh Plan Guidelines

The seventh five year plan adopted the following policy towards the sugar industry:

1. Sectoral priorities i.e. co-operative, public sector, in that order, should be followed as in earlier plan.
2. Basic criterion for establishment of new sugar factory would be abundant availability of cane in compact area around the proposed factory site.
3. To ensure adequate supply of cane to the existing units as well as to meet the needs for further expansion, no licenses would be granted for setting up a new factory within radius of 40 km of existing unit.
4. To take advantage of economies of scale; to incorporate modern technology subject to availability of cane, new units would be licensed for an initial capacity of 2500 TCD, expansion of existing units up to 5000 TCD will be permitted only if the entire additional cane requirement accrues through increased productivity and not by expansion of area under cane cultivation.
5. Establishment of new sugar units in backward areas may be given priority subject to adequate cane availability and socio-economic feasibility. The backward areas are likely to get very little advantage of this policy since adequate availability of cane in these areas before setting up sugar factory would be remote possibility in these areas[6].
6. State Government/Sugar Factories would be advised to intensify programmes for cane development. Sugar factories can also avail themselves of loan facilities available on soft term for cane development from Sugar Development Fund (SDF).

The seventh plan guidelines thus ensure that we should have sugarcane first; and not sugar factories first. This policy was formulated in order to reduce the problem of sickness of sugar factories and make them viable right from the beginning and also to check the tendency to set up small units without adequate supply of cane.

For financing of these new units and expansion of capacity, we shall review the government policy with regard to financing of sugar factories in the next section.

Revised Guidelines of 1990

By the end of Seventh Five Year Plan the Government of India has revised the guidelines for licensing of new factories and expansion of existing sugar factories. The Government formulated the following revised guidelines which are applicable during the period of Eighth Five Year Plan[7] (1991-92 to 1996-97).

1. **Crushing Capacity–Daily Tonnes Crushing Capacity:** New sugar factories will continue to be licensed for a minimum crushing capacity of 2500 TCD. There will not be any maximum limit on such a capacity. However, in the areas specified as industrially backward by the Government of India and certified by the Indian Council of Agricultural Research to be agroclimatically suited for development of sugarcane, licensing of new sugar factories in the cooperative and public sectors would be allowed for an initial capacity of 1750 TCD, subject to the condition that units would expand their capacity to 2500 TCD within a period of 5 years of going into production.
2. **Distance:** Licenses for new sugar factories will be issued subject to the condition that the distance between the proposed new sugar factory and an existing / already licensed sugar factory should be 25 kms. This distance criterion of 25 kms could, however, be relaxed to 15 kms in special cases where cane availability so justifies.
3. **Viability:** The basic criterion for grant of licenses for new sugar units would be their viability, mainly from the point of view of cane availability and potentiality for development of sugarcane.
4. **Cane Price:** All the licenses will be issued with the condition that cane price will be payable on the basis of sugarcane content of the sugarcane.
5. **Preference:** Other things being equal, preference in licensing will be given to proposals from the cooperative sector and the public sector. In case more than one

application is received from any zone of operation, priority will be given to the application received earlier. However, in such cases also preference will be given to the cooperative sector, followed by the public sector and the private sector.

6. **Expansion:** Priority will continue to be given to sugar factory with capacity less than 2500 TCD to expand to the aforesaid minimum crushing capacity.
7. **Period:** While granting licenses for new units and expansion projects, the additional capacity to be created up to the end of eighth plan i.e. 1996-97 will be kept in view.

GOVERNMENT POLICY TOWARDS FINANCING OF SUGAR FACTORIES

Prior to 1952, most of the sugar factories were in the private or joint sector. Later, the Government of India followed the ideology of building up co-operative sector as an integral part of economic planning in India. In order to promote setting up of co-operative sugar factories, a scheme of financing co-operative sugar factories was evolved, under which the state government participates in the share capital of co-operative factories and the central and the state governments are to guarantee the loans advanced to the factories by the financial institutions like Industrial Finance Corporation of India (IFCI), Industrial Credit and Investment Corporation of India (ICICI) and Industrial Development Bank of India (IDBI).

To enable the state governments to participate in the share capital of the sugar factories, National Cooperative Development Corporation (NCDC) advances loans to them, out of the funds placed at its disposal by the central government.

The pattern of financing a new sugar factory is as follows[8]:

> The state government's minimum contribution to share capital per factory is 10 per cent of the project cost. The

state government's contribution over and above the minimum contribution is partly financed by NCDC. This contribution of NCDC in the share capital is 50 per cent of the state's share capital above the minimum contribution, if the factory is located in 'developed area', whereas the NCDC contributes a higher percentage-65 per cent, if the factory is located in under developed area.

As a result of the considerable assistance and encouragement provided by the government and the central financial institutions, the number of co-operative factories in the country has increased considerably.

At the same time, it must be noted that, NCDC is the only organization at national level which provides risk capital and margin money to co-operatives for expanding their business operations. Since 1963, NCDC has played a pivotal role in the task of building the country's economy through co-operatives. At times, when inflow of assistance from central financial institutions is restricted, NCDC steps in to provide a part of assistance, so that, the pace of installation is not adversely affected. NCDC ensures the completion of new units within a stipulated period of 39 months.

PRICING POLICY

The pricing policy towards sugar industry can be examined in two parts namely (i) pricing of sugarcane, and (ii) pricing of sugar.

Pricing of Sugarcane: Sugarcane prices is a very important policy variable because cane prices play an important role in the farmer's decision to increase the area under cane cultivation and thus production of sugarcane. The Government in 1934, on the demand of the cane growers, passed the sugarcane resolution which conferred powers on the provincial (state) governments to fix minimum price of cane. The minimum price of cane continued to be fixed by the state governments upto 1950-51. But the lack of uniformity in the methodology adopted in fixing the prices, led to unrest among cane growers in the country. So, at the request of Government of India, the Tariff Board (1950) examined the issue and suggested that while fixing minimum price, cost of cane cultivation, fair return to cane cultivator should be taken into consideration. Accordingly provision was made in 1955 to empower the Central Government to fix the minimum price of cane on the basis of following:

(a) Cost of production of sugarcane.

(b) The return to the grower from alternative crops and trend of prices of agricultural commodities.

(c) The availability of sugar to consumer at a fair price.

(d) Recovery of sugar from sugarcane.

Since 1962-63, the government policy has been to link the statutory minimum price of sugarcane to the basic sugar recovery percentage with a premium on every 0.1 per cent rise in the recovery over the basic recovery. While fixing the cane prices, the government is guided by the recommendations of the Agricultural Prices Commission and state governments and also the views of the cane growers and sugar industry. Thus, the minimum cane price is being fixed by the central government, with the object of ensuring payment of a guaranteed price for cane by sugar factories to the cane growers[9].

Table 1 gives the statutory minimum price of cane linked to basic recovery and also the premium on higher recovery for the period 1963-2002. The cane growers were not satisfied with their formula of cane prices. Therefore, in addition to the statutory minimum price of cane announced by tho Government of India, the state governments were also empowered to decide the cane price higher than the price announced by the central government. Thus, the farmers were assured of remunerative price for the cane crop.

However, it should be noted that, irrespective of cane prices announced by the state governments, the calculation of the levy price of sugar is made on the basis of the statutory minimum price of cane announced by the central government.

Table 1
The Statutory Minimum Price of Sugarcane

Years	*Minimum price (Rs. per quintal)*	*Linked to basic recovery*	*Premium on every 0.1% increase (Rs per quintal)*
1963-64	4.69	9.0	0.04
1964-66	5.36	10.4	0.04
1966-67	5.68	9.4	0.04
1967-70	7.37	9.4	0.05
1970-72	7.37	9.4	0.07
1972-74	8.00	8.5	0.09
1974-78	8.5	8.5	0.10
1978-79	10.0	8.5	0.12
1979-80	12.5	8.5	0.15
1980-83	13.0	8.5	0.15
1983-84	13.5	8.5	0.16
1984-85	14.0	8.5	0.16
1985-86	16.5	8.5	0.19
1986-87	17.0	8.5	0.20
1987-88	18.5	8.5	0.22
1988-89	19.5	8.5	0.23
1989-90	22.00	8.5	0.26
1990-91	23.0	8.5	0.27
1991-92	26.0	8.5	0.30
1992-93	31.0	8.5	0.36
1993-94	34.5	8.5	0.40
1994-95	39.1	8.5	0.46
1995-96	42.5	8.5	0.54
1996-97	45.9	8.5	0.57
1997-98	48.5	8.5	0.60
1998-99	52.7	8.5	0.62
1999-00	56.1	8.5	0.66
2000-01	59.50	8.5	0.70
2001-02	62.05	8.5	0.73

Sources: 1. Bharatiya Sugar Directory, 1987.
2. Co-operative Sugar, March, 2002, Vol. 33, No. 7.

Sugar Prices

Before 1942, the price of sugar was determined by the market forces of supply and demand. During the World War-II period, there was acute shortage of sugar. Therefore, in April

1942, Government of India issued the sugar control order[10]. Under this order, no sugar factory was permitted to sell its sugar to persons other than those authorized by sugar controller.

After independence, the "Indian Sugar Syndicate" was formed. This became the sole selling organization under the power vested by the Essential Supplies Act, 1949[11]. Later on, in 1952-53, "Directorate of Sugar" was set up by the Government of India and control of sugar price and distribution was taken over by the central government. Whenever the sugar production in the country decreased and the sugar stocks were low, the government imposed control on sugar release and price. On the other hand, when the sugar production was more than the expected level, the government did not fix any ex-factory price of sugar.

In 1958, the government adopted other measures for effective control on availability of sugar to all the people. Some of the important measures adopted by the government were[12]:

(a) Licensing of wholesale dealers in sugar by the state government.

(b) Assigning of specific quota to individual states.

(c) Banning inter-state movements of sugar.

The government policies of control on price and on distribution of sugar have been mainly governed by the amount of sugar produced in a given year with a view to enable the consumer to purchase sugar at reasonable price.

The fixing of ex-factory prices sets a limitation on the price payable to the raw material i.e. sugarcane. During the period of control of sugar prices, the cane prices did not exceed the minimum statutory price of cane. This price of cane was not very remunerative. Hence, there was a decline in the area under sugarcane cultivation and consequently the sugarcane output. This, in turn, affected the sugar production. It was feared that due to the controls imposed by the government on the sugar industry, the production of sugar may fall sharply and may even fall short of internal demand.

So, it was realized that, in order to induce the farmers to cultivate cane, higher cane price than the minimum statutory price should be paid. This was not possible under ex-factory sugar price control. Therefore, in 1967, a system of partial decontrol of sugar was announced.

Under this partial control policy, 60 per cent of the production of sugar was procured by the government at a fixed levy price, for public distribution system. Factories were free to sell remaining output in the free market, subject to the releases from the factories to be sanctioned by the government. The "levy price" is calculated on the basis of statutory minimum price of cane.

The sale of 40 per cent of the sugar output at a price higher than the levy price enabled the factories to pay higher cane prices to the farmers and attract more cane. The policy of partial control thus attracted more cane growers and sugar output showed an increase in the year 1969-70.

The "levy price" of sugar is fixed with the help of committee of technical and costing experts. The committee refers to the data on cost of production of sugar in different agro-climatic regions for the three seasons.

The important components of cost of production are :

1. Cost of cane.
2. Fuel, power, etc.
3. Salary and wages, factory repairs, etc.

After considering the above mentioned factors of cost of production, the government fixes the levy price of sugar for different zones.

The government has continued with this policy of partial control and varied the proportion of levy and free sale sugar depending on the circumstance in the given year. Table 2 depicts the sugar price policy over the years and the levy-free sale proportions decided by the government, which changed according to circumstances.

Table 2
Sugar pricing policy in India - 1941-42 to 2001-2002

Years	*Policy*	*Levy %*	*Free sale %*
1941-47	Control	-	-
1947-49	De-control	-	-
1949-50	Control	-	-
1950-52	Partial control	-	-
1952-58	De-control	-	-
1958-61	Control	-	-
1961-63	De-control	-	-
1963-67	Control	-	-
1967-68	Partial control	60	40
1968-70	Partial control	70	30
1970-72	Partial control	60	40
1972-74	Partial control	70	30
1974-75	Partial control	65	35
1985-86	Partial control	55	45
1986-88	Partial control	50	50
1988-90	Partial control	45	55
1990-92	Partial control	45	55
1992-96	Partial control	40	60
1996-97	Partial control	40	60
1997-98	Partial control	40	60
1998-99	Partial control	40	60
1999-00	Partial control	30	70
2000-01	Partial control	30	70
2001-02	Partial control	15	85

Sources: 1. Bharatiya Sugar Directory, 1987.
2. Co-operative Sugar, March, 2002, Vol. 33, No 7

RECENT SCHEMES FOR DEVELOPMENT OF SUGAR INDUSTRY

Due to the inflationary factors, there has been unprecedented rise in the cost of plant and machinery. This to some extent set a limitation to growth of new factories and expansion of existing factories. Very often, there is a gap between licensed capacity and installed capacity due to the rising cost of plant and machinery. To assess the situation, Government of India appointed a committee under the chairmanship of Shri S.V. Sampath in 1973. The objectives were:

1. To examine the cost of establishing a new sugar factory of 1250 TCD and suggest ways and means of reducing the total cost of such project.
2. To suggest minimum economic size of new sugar factories in the context of rising costs.
3. To suggest various incentives and other measures for making new sugar factories economically viable.

This committee classified the cane growing area into three categories:

(a) Low recovery area–area where average recovery of sugar was below 9.0 per cent.

(b) Medium recovery area–where recovery of sugar is in between 9 and 10 per cent.

(c) High recovery area–where average recovery of sugar is above 10 per cent consistently.

The committee suggested various incentives for new sugar factories as well as expansion projects.

The committee prescribed various concessions to a new sugar factory for the first five crushing seasons. Concessions are given to new sugar factories as regards to the free sale quota of the sugar output for the initial five years of production.

The free sale quota is higher in the initial years and is gradually brought on par with the other factories. Also, the quota varies with the recovery zones; highest free sale quota for the low recovery zone and lowest for the high recovery zone; as well as the plant cost. Similarly, higher free sale quotas were also allowed for the units that expanded the installed capacity. Under this scheme also, higher incentives were given to the sugar factories in the low recovery areas. A large number of factories have taken advantage of this incentive scheme since 1975. With the change of sugar price from time to time and consequent changes in the levy free sale ratios, excise-rebates etc., the Sampath committee scheme of incentives was also modified as per the requirement from time to time.

SUGARCANE DEVELOPMENT FUND ACT OF 1982

To facilitate rehabilitation and modernization of the sugar industry and for making grants for the purpose of any research project aimed at the development of sugar industry, the Government of India had enacted two acts namely, The Sugar Research Act 1982 and The Sugarcane Development Fund Act 1982[13]. These acts empowered the Government of India to collect cess at the rate not exceeding Rs 10/- per quintal of sugar. The cess so collected is credited to the consolidated fund of India and utilized for following purposes:

1. Loan for modernization and rehabilitation,
2. Loan for sugarcane development,
3. Grants for research and
4. For maintenance of buffer stocks.

Thus, as a result of the commendable efforts on part of Government of India, sugar industry has made a rapid progress during the last 4 decades.

From the table 3, it is clear that there are variations in the price recommended by Agricultural Price Commission (CACP) and SMP fixed by the Government of India. For example, in the initial years i.e. from 1967-68 to 1970-71, the prices fixed by the government are slightly higher than the prices recommended by CACP. During the years 1975-76, 1976-77 and 1977-78, the prices fixed by the government were lower than the CACP prices. This might be due to bumper sugarcane crop during these years. Similar situation prevailed even during the years 1981-82 to 1984-85. After 1985-86, the situation was reverse as the SMP fixed by the government were higher than the CACP prices with the exception of years 1990-91, 1991-92, 1993-94 and 1994-95. In these years CACP prices were higher than the SMP fixed by the government.

POLICY OF THE MAHARASHTRA STATE GOVERNMENT

It may be stated that the State Government of Maharashtra has not spelt out the clear policy of establishment of new

Table 3
Price of Sugarcane Recommended by CACP and SMP fixed by the Government of India.

Year	*Price recommended by CACP (Rs. per quintal)*	*SMP fixed by the Central Government (Rs. per quintal)*
1967-68	5.68	7.37
1968-69	7.23	7.37
1969-70	7.27	7.37
1970-71	7.35	7.37
1971-72	7.37	7.37
1972-73	8.00	8.00
1973-74	8.00	8.00
1974-75	8.50	8.50
1975-76	9.50	8.50
1976-77	9.50	8.50
1977-78	9.50	8.50
1978-79	10.00	10.00
1979-80	10.00	12.50
1980-81	13.00	13.00
1981-82	15.50	13.00
1982-83	15.50	13.00
1983-84	16.00	14.00
1984-85	16.00	14.00
1985-86	16.50	16.50
1986-87	-	17.00
1987-88	17.45	18.50
1988-89	19.00	19.50
1989-90	20.00	22.00
1990-91	23.00	23.00
1991-92	26.00	26.00
1992-93	29.00	31.00
1993-94	36.50	34.50
1994-95	39.50	39.10
1995-96	42.50	42.50
1996-97	45.90	45.90
1997-98	48.45	48.45
1998-99	52.70	52.70
1999-00	56.10	56.10
2000-01	59.50	59.50
2001-02	62.05	—

Sources: 1. Co-operative Sugar, March, 2002, Vol. 33 No.7.
2. Various Issues of Annual Reports of Maharashtra Rajya Sahakari Sakhar Karkhana Sangh Ltd. (1976-77 to 1995-96).

sugar factories and the expansion of existing units, in the form of any policy declaration. However, the policy of the State Government in promoting new sugar factories and in expansion of existing units is reflected in its various decisions about these points. The first proposal of the sugar factory in cooperative sector was cleared by the State Government in the year 1948. It was the proposal of Pravara Cooperative Sugar Factory at Loni in Ahmednagar district. Thereafter, the licensing of sugar factories was started in 1951 by Government of India, the state government recommended the proposals of sugar factories in cooperative sector only. The efforts of the state government in getting the licenses to these proposals from Government of India reflects on the policy of the state government to promote the sugar factories in cooperative sector.

The State Government had appointed the committee of experts in 1980 for making recommendations for the formation of zones for drawl of sugarcane by sugar factories in Maharashtra state. The committee noted that many disadvantages emanated from overlapping areas, such as concrete steps for sugarcane development cannot be taken by the concerned sugar factories, the possibility of diversion of sugarcane to the factory offering more attractive terms and crisscross movement of the sugarcane resulting in higher incidence of transport cost.

The committee came to the conclusion that it would be practically impossible to device any scheme of zoning based on dismemberment of cane growing farmers and converting their status into non-members[13]. This committee submitted its report in 1983 and based on the recommendations of this committee, the State Government has issued the Maharashtra Sugar Factories (Reservation of areas and regulation of crushing and sugarcane supply) Order 1984, providing for zoning of areas of sugarcane for sugar factories in the state. The State Government has thus taken effective steps to allocate the specific zones for the sugar factories in the state to ensure adequate supply of cane to these factories from the specified areas.

Though the state Government of Maharashtra has demarcated zones of sugarcane for sugar factories in Maharashtra, in the past many cooperative sugar factories were located in this state without considering the adequate cane availability to the new unit. This has created the position of overlapping of areas in two or more than two sugar factories. To quote the study team to look into the problem relating to inadequate supply of sugarcane to sugar factories in Maharashtra. The team observed with great concern that of late, the sugar factories in the cooperative sector in Maharashtra have come in a haphazard manner without having full regard and proper assessment of the position of sugarcane availability in the areas operated by these factories. In fact, while recommending applications for issue of licenses and later while setting up some of these licensed factories, no attempt was made to allocate and demarcate clear cut zones of operation to such factories and no proper assessment of cane availability position was made[14].

The state government observed that the recommendations made by the earlier committee, popularly known as the Gulabrao Patil Committee, which were accepted by it under its Resolution No. SSK-1783/3-3535/(206)/3-6, dated 28th March 1985, were not adequate to bring the desired results in rehabilitating the sick cooperative sugar factories and the state government had therefore been forced to take ad-hoc decisions from time to time like giving interim loans, postponement of recoveries of government dues and reschedulement of dues of other financing agencies, giving of government guarantees etc.

In spite of government's acceptance of the Gulabrao Patil Committee report, the trend of sickness was not arrested. Out of the measures recommended, only few were actually implemented. During this period the sugar industry in the country passed through very bad period and sickness in all states with exception of Tamil Nadu. This prompted the Reserve Bank of India to appoint a study group to analyse the causes of sickness and to suggest remedial measures. The State Government, however, felt that there should be a clear and definite policy in this behalf and therefore appointed the present committee under the chairmanship of Shri Shivajirao Patil in May 1987, with the constitution and terms of reference as embodied therein.

RECOMMENDATIONS OF THE HIGH POWERED COMMITTEE ON SUGAR INDUSTRY

The high powered committee on sugar industry submitted its report to government on 24th April 1997. The Report was presented to the honourable food minister Shri S.S. Barnala by Shri B.B. Mahajan, chairman of the committee.

The Committee was set up by the Ministry of Food on 14th March 1997 in pursuance of a directive by Allahabad High Court in a writ petition challenging the power of the state government to advise the sugar mills on the cane price payable to the can growers with the following terms and references:

1. To study the development and growth of sugar industry in India vis-à-vis other sugar producing countries.
2. To study the laws and rules and regulations relating to sugar industry in India and other sugar producing countries.
3. To suggest modifications, amendments and repeal of any existing law and controls with a view to ensure healthy growth and development of the sugar industry, and building a healthy relationship between the farmers and the industry.
4. To suggest ways and means to increase production and efficiency through modernisation so that sugar is available to the general public at reasonable prices.
5. To suggest methods for increasing productivity of sugarcane and way to ensure fair and remunerative prices to sugarcane growers.

The names of representatives of various organizations were received on 24th April 1997. The Committee started its work from that date. The committee issued a public notice inviting suggestions on its terms of reference followed by questionnaire to various organizations and state governments. The teams of the committee visited the major sugar producing states namely, Maharashtra, Gujarat, Karnataka, Andhra Pradesh, Tamil Nadu, Uttar Pradesh, Bihar, Punjab and Haryana. During these visits the teams held discussions with the representatives of the cane growers, mill managements and state governments. They also visited various institutions conducting research in sugarcane and sugar manufacturing and held discussions with the scientists at those institutes. Thereafter, the Committee held discussions with the state governments, representatives of cane growers, sugar industry, research institutes for sugarcane and sugar manufacture and other concerned organizations. It also held discussions with the concerned Department of Central Government and relevant industrial organizations on specific issues. The Committee also studied the development of sugar industry and laws and practices relating to the sugar industry, trade and sugarcane cultivation in twelve important sugarcane producing countries viz., Australia, South Africa, Sri Lanka, Taiwan, Thailand and USA on the basis of information received from the concerned organization in those countries in response to the questionnaires sent by the Committee and other relevant available information. A small team of the Committee also visited four important sugar producing countries viz., Thailand, Australia, South Africa and Mauritius to study the working of the industry in those countries and had discussions with the representatives of the cane growers, mill managements and government authorised research scientists in those countries.

The Committee has considered the various policy issues and institutional framework relating to sugar industry, trade and sugarcane cultivation in India in the light of the replies received to questionnaires, discussion with the concerned organizations and the practices prevailing in the other countries. It has made recommendation on various policy matters and institutional arrangements which in opinion of the committee will lead to the development of the industry on healthy lines in the long term interest of the industry, cane growers and the consumers and help to meet the challenge of global competition.

The report of the Committee is unanimous and there is no minute of descent.

The Committee has recommended complete decontrol of sugar price as in the opinion of the Committee the present system of partial control leads to higher market price for free-sale sugar as the mill have to compensate themselves for loss that incurred in supplying 40 per cent of the production in levy at the below cost price. This puts the domestic sugar industry at a disadvantage vis-à-vis imports and discourage exports, aggravates cyclical fluctuations in production as the sugar mills are unable to compete with Khandsari units during the period of lower cane production so that small percentage of limited cane supplies become available to the mills. The dual price system in the opinion of the Committee also encourages setting up of mills in high cost areas thereby building up of a high cost sugar industry. It is the principal reason for the poor financial health of industry and for investment in the industry not forthcoming without special incentives and it also leads to widespread resentment among cane growers as they feel that they have to bear the burden of subsidy for sugar in public distribution system unlike other commodities where the burden of subsidy is borne by the government. The committee has however recommended the phasing of decontrol over a period of two years to allow time to such factories as have set up in relatively high cost areas due to advantage of high levy price under the system of partial control to take necessary steps to improve their efficiency so that they can face the competition. It has also suggested that control on releases should continue even after complete decontrol of sugar prices in the interest of stability of sugar prices.

The Committee has recommended that supply of sugar through Public Distribution System (PDS) may be discontinued when complete decontrol became effective, as there are large-scale leakage of levy sugar into open market, large percentage of subsidy is availed of by the non-poor and even where sugar reaches the card holders its financial benefit is very small. The poor consumers in the rural areas are in fact the net losers as they consume mainly gur / jaggery whose prices move in tandem with price of free-sale sugar and would therefore be higher than they would be under a system of complete decontrol. The Committee has expressed the view that the subsidy at present allowed in supply of sugar through Public Distribution System can be distributed among the beneficiaries by adding to the subsidy at present allowed on foodgrains. It was suggested that if Government nevertheless wishes to continue supply of sugar under Public Distribution System, the required quantity may be purchased from industry or trade by tendering or at fixed prices from the mills as adopted by banks for valuation of sugar study for working capital loans. It has expressed the view that the additional subsidy would be offset to some extent by higher realisation from excise duty on larger quantum of free-sale sugar on which excise duties are higher than on levy sugar and if there is still any deficiency the balance may be met by suitable increase in excise duty on sugar.

The committee has recommended that announcement of statutory minimum price for sugarcane should be continued even under system of complete decontrol on sugar prices as a guarantee of a minimum price to the growers. It was however suggested that the statutory minimum price (SMP) should be based mainly on the cost of production of sugarcane and return to the growers from alternative crops and should be delinked from the price of sugar in the market. It was also recommended that instead of linking SMP to percentage of recovery of sugar, which is also influenced by the state of machinery and the operational efficiency of the mill, it may be linked to the sugar content of cane supplied by growers to the mills and a premium may be allowed on the varieties which have higher sugar content.

So far as actual cane price payable to the growers is concerned the committee has recommended a fixed share for the growers in the sale realisation from the sale of sugar as is the practice in most of the major sugar producing countries in the world. It was suggested that the share of growers may be fixed on the percentage of average cost of purchase of sugarcane to total sales realisation from sale of sugar (excluding excise duty and cess and incidence of purchase and other taxes levied on sugarcane by state government) during the last ten years. Cane price will be fixed separately for different zones formed, but on the basis of level of sugar prices and recovery percentage of sugar. Within a zone all mills will be required to pay the same price. The growers in a zone with higher average recovery than all India average will get proportionately higher cane price as factories in such zone will have relatively higher capacity to pay.

The committee has recommended the setting up of a sugarcane pricing board comprising an economist of repute as chairman and senior officers from Departments of Sugar, Civil Supplies and Ministry of Agriculture, Economic Advisor in the Ministry of Finance, one representative each from the two apex organizations of the industry viz., National Federation of Cooperative Sugar Factories and Indian Sugar Mills Association and two representatives of cane growers, one from the tropical zone and another from the sub-tropical zone to be nominated by Government of India as members. The Board will determine in September each year advance price for ensuing crushing season on the basis of likely sugar prices and final price for each zone will be determined by the Board before the end of November next based on the actual ex-factory sale price. The Committee has recommended that the mills should be statutorily required to pay minimum of 80 per cent of the advance price determined by the Board within fifteen days of supply of cane by the growers and the remaining amount before the end of the sugar season. The difference between the advance price and final price shall be paid by the mills within fifteen days of announcement of final price. It has suggested for a provision being made in all the states for recovery of arrears of sugarcane prices remaining unpaid till the end of sugar season as arrears of land revenue besides payments of interest at the rate of 15 per cent on any delay in payment. The committee has suggested that the cooperative sugar mills in Maharashtra, Gujarat and North Karnataka may continue the present practice of distributing the sale proceeds amongst the member growers if they so desire and the cooperative mills in other states in which growers have majority of share capital may also be free to adopt that system at their option.

The committee has recommended that the existing policy for licensing of new sugar mills may continue with certain modifications as the same is necessary to ensure that new sugar factories are not installed very close to the existing sugar factories which would adversely affect the financial viability of the latter and also discourage the factories from investing in cane development in their area. They have however suggested that there should be no need for a license for expansion in capacity although applications for allocation of additional cane area where required will have to be made to the state government concerned before expansion is undertaken.

The committee has recommended continuance of the existing system of cane area reservation under which all cane growers in the reserved area of the mill are required to supply cane to the specified mill and the mill is obliged to crush all the cane bonded by the growers from the reserved area for supply to the mill. It has come to the conclusion that in the absence of this system, it will be difficult for sugar factories to regulate the supply of cane by the farmers according to the crushing capacity available on each day, resulting in inadequate sugarcane available on some days and excessive cane coming to the mill on other days leading to long waiting period for the growers, some of whom may have to carry their cane to distant mills for disposal involving higher transportation cost as well as driage of cane. The system is also in the view of the committee, necessary to provide incentive to the mills to undertake cane development. The committee has made a number of recommendations to strengthen the system and make it more equitable. In order to strengthen the incentive for cane development by the mills, it was recommended that reservation of area should be on permanent basis and any area should be transferred from reserved area of a factory to another only if cane availability in its area is surplus to its requirement for its existing capacity including expansion under implementation.

In order to provide dis-incentive against neglect of cane development by any factory it was suggested that if the per hectare yield of cane in the reserved area of a factory is lower than the average in other similar areas due to insufficient cane development work, the availability of cane in the reserved area may be based on the average in similar areas.

The committee has suggested that mills in all states should be free to have direct link with farmers as regards cane supply, payment of cane price and cane development. It has however recommended the setting up of an organization in the area of each mill to represent the interests of growers.

The committee has expressed the view that the Indian sugar industry is generally competitive and given a proper policy environment it should be able to face competition from the foreign producers. It has accordingly recommended that the sugar may continue to be on OGL to protect the consumers against any undue rise in price and provide stimulus competition to sugar mills to minimise cost. However, in order to provide a level playing field to the domestic producers it has recommended that import duty may be levied at 40 per cent of average difference between ex-factory price of free-sale and levy sugar during the past five years so long as the system of partial control continues. This would amount to about Rs. 130/- per quintal. It has also suggested counter veiling duty of Rs. 85/- per quintal to cover excise duty and cess on sugar levied by Government of India of Rs. 50/- per quintal to cover incidence of taxes on purchase of sugarcane levied by coastal states.

The committee has recommended a regular annual export quota of one million tonnes of sugar so that the industry can plan properly by way of setting up of extra capacity, organizing production of export quality and building markets. Additional quota may be released after the end of April when production estimates have formed up in installments not exceeding one million tonnes at a time so as to not to disturb the market.

The committee has recommended abolition of the scheme of incentives, under which the new sugar mills were allowed exemption from levy for 5-8 years and the factories undertaking expansion from levy on the additional production for 5 years, in the case of letters of intent to be issued in future and have suggested that efforts should instead be made to make the industry financially viable to attract investments. The Committee has come to the conclusion that while the schemes have played useful role in the past in attracting investment for setting up new sugar mills and expansion of capacity of existing mills, it adversely affects the existing units particularly those in the vicinity of new units and encourages setting up of new units instead of expansion of existing units which is more economical than setting up of new units in areas where cost of production of sugar is comparatively higher. It has also tended to encourage the setting up of large number of smaller capacity plants and prevent the industry from fully utilizing the economies of scale. The Committee has however recommended that on grounds of equity incentive should be allowed to those units which are at present enjoying such benefit for the balance period of their entitlement and also to new units where letters of intents are issued before the issue of government orders for dis-continuance of the scheme. The committee has suggested that after decontrol of sugar prices these units may be compensated by appropriate grant from the Sugar Development Fund for the period provided in the present scheme in case of new units and expansion projects or for the balance period under the relevant scheme in case of units which have already availed of incentives for sometime. It has also suggested that if there is any difficulty in compensating this loss from the Sugar Development Fund (SDF), the expenditure may be met by levy of a specific cess for the purpose for a limited period during which the grants are payable.

The committee has recommended that no new licence for khandsari unit should be allowed within reserved area of a sugar mill and within 25 kms from the site of a sugar mill so that sugarcane produced within this area is available to the mill for crushing and loss in sugar production involved on account of its crushing by khandsari units which have low sugar recovery is avoided. It has however recommended that khandsari units located outside the area of the sugar mill may be allowed to install vacuum pan and modernise and expand without any restrictions. However units with crushing capacity in excess of 500 tonnes per day may be required to supply sugar under levy subject to incentives available to new units and may also be required to pay excise duty at 50 per cent of that imposed on sugar. It has also made a number of recommendations for technical upgradation of khandsari and gur industry.

The committee has recommended the abolition of the present system of licensing of wholesale dealers in sugar and existing restrictions on stock-holding limits and period of turnover as in its opinion these serve no useful purpose and are counterproductive.

The committee has made a number of recommendations for strengthening the research and development efforts for sugarcane cultivation as well as sugar industry, and stronger association of the industry and growers to ensure that research and development efforts effectively help the industry and the growers for reducing cost of production of sugar, better utilization of by-products of the industry and dealing with the problem of sickness, particularly in the cooperative sector. It has also made recommendations for reducing the magnitude of cyclical fluctuations in production of sugar and recommended maintenance of buffer-stock on a regular basis. It has also made recommendations for more effective utilization of the funds available in the Sugar Development Fund for promoting research and development efforts in sugarcane cultivation and sugar industry, development of sugarcane cultivation by the factories, rehabilitation of sick sugar mills and helping the factories to install necessary pollution control measures[15].

To sum up, the government policy regulates almost every aspect of sugar industry such as regulation and pricing of sugarcane, quality, storage, and release of sugar stocks, control over price and distribution of by-products like molasses and alcohol, regulation of wages etc. Similarly financing of sugar industry, be it for financing of new projects of credit facilities for other purpose like purchase of cane, stock of sugar etc. is severely controlled by the financial institutions and banks under overall directions from Government of India and Reserve Bank of India. Even with regard to the sale of free quota sugar its release, trading and stocking by the traders, the regulations are so severe that not much is left for the market speculation.

As mentioned earlier, the targets of licensing of sugar factories depend upon a number of factors like requirement of sugar for internal consumption, exports and buffer stocks. These requirements decide as to how many new licenses and how many licenses for expansion are to be given.

The 7th plan guidelines ensured that we should have sugar cane first, and not sugar factories first. This policy was formulated in order to reduce the problem of sickness of sugar factories and make them viable right from the beginning and also to check the tendency to set up small units without adequate supply of cane. Thus the minimum cane price is being fixed by the central government, with the object of ensuring payment of a guaranteed price for cane by sugar factories to the cane growers.

The levy price of sugar is fixed with the help of committee of technical and costing experts. The committee refers to the data on cost of production of sugar in different agro-climatic regions for the three seasons.

The Sampath Committee scheme of incentives was also modified as per the requirement from time to time. The committee came to the conclusion that it would be practically impossible to device any scheme of zoning based on dismemberment of cane growing farmers and converting their status into non-member. The state government however felt that there should be a clear definite policy in this behalf and therefore appointed the present committee under the chairmanship of Shri Shivajirao Patil, in May 1987, with the constitution and terms of reference as embodied therein. So far as actual cane price payable to the growers is concerned the committee has recommended a fixed share for the growers in the sale realisation from the sale of sugar as is the practice in most of the major sugar producing countries in the world.

The committee has made a number of recommendations for strengthening the research and development efforts for sugarcane cultivation as well as sugar industry, and stronger association of the industry and growers to ensure that research and development efforts effectively help the industry and the growers for reducing cost of production of sugar, better utilization of by-products of the industry and dealing with the problem of sickness, particularly in the cooperative sector. It has also made recommendations for more effective utilization of the funds available in the Sugar Development Fund for promoting research and development efforts in sugarcane cultivation and sugar industry, development of sugarcane cultivation by the factories, rehabilitation of sick sugar mills and helping the factories to install necessary pollution control measures.

References

1. Singh R.S., India's Sugar Industry, 1997.

2. Report of Sugar Enquiry Commission, Government of India, 1965, p. 137.
3. *Ibid.*, p. 139.
4. Sixth Five Year Plan, Planning Commission, Government of India, 1980-85.
5. Kharche R.M., Sugar Cooperatives in Developing Economy, Parimal Prakashan, Aurangabad, 1988.
6. *Ibid.*, p. 61.
7. Cooperative Sugar, Vol. 23, No. 10, Published by NFCFFC, New Delhi, June, 1992, pp. 591-96.
8. Manoharrao P. J., Bharatiya Sugar Directory, 1987-88, p. 39.
9. Manoharrao P.J., Development of Indian Sugar Industry – Historical, Bharatiya Sugar Directory, 1987, p. 9.
10. *Ibid.*, p. 20.
11. *Ibid.*, p. 20.
12. *Ibid.*, p. 20.
13. Report of the Committee of Experts for Making Recommendations for Formation of Zones the drawl of Sugarcane by Sugar Factories in Maharashtra, Bombay, 1983.
14. Letter No. F. 27(C) 5-ST, dated 6th December , 1975, Government of India, Ministry of Agriculture and Irrigation (Department of Food), Directorate of Sugar and Vanaspati, Krishi Bhavan, New Delhi.
15. Letter No. F. 12-109 / 98-SP dated 20 April 1998, National Federation of Cooperative Sugar Factories Limited Vaikunth, III Floor, 82-83, Nehru Palace, New Delhi.

4

Growth Trends in Area, Yield, Production and Prices of Sugarcane

Sugarcane and its main products are known in India since ancient times. The earliest reference of sugar appears in Atharva Veda, the sacred book of Hindus composed between 5000 and 1000 B.C. Efforts to establish a modern sugar industry however go back only to the beginning of the twentieth century. India lies entirely to the north of equator. Hence, sugarcane is grown in nearly all parts of India[1].

Sugarcane crop is grown in several rainfall, temperature and soil regions. However, sugarcane growing area could be grouped into sub-tropical and tropical belt[2]. The states of Maharashtra, Gujarat, Andhra Pradesh, Tamil Nadu and Kerala comprise the 'tropical region' while the states of Punjab, Uttar Pradesh, Bihar and West Bengal comprise the 'sub-tropical' region.

India is the largest producer of sugarcane in the world. There has been considerable importance to this commercial crop during the last two decades[3]. In the year 2003-04 at all India level, the area under sugarcane was 39.95 lakh hectares and production 2362 lakh tonnes with an average yield of 59.10 tonnes.[4]

Maharashtra is one of the leading sugarcane growing states in India. It is a perennial irrigated crop grown in all the zones of the state. Maharashtra State occupied a well recognised place of pride on the sugarcane map of the country. The area under sugarcane in the Maharashtra state is 5.26 lakh hectares and have total production of 269.82 lakh tonnes with an average yield of 51.30 tonnes per hectare in the year 2003-04[5].

The area under sugarcane in Maharashtra is concentrated in low rainfall regions in the eastern part of the Sahyadri mountains. Pune division i.e. Ahmednagar, Pune and Solapur districts; Kolhapur division i.e. Satara, Sangli and Kolhapur districts; and Nasik district are the major sugarcane growing districts of the state with 71.96 per cent of the state area. Some districts of Marathwada i.e. Aurangabad and Osmanabad have moderate area under sugarcane i.e. 9.60 per cent of the state area[6].

In this chapter an attempt is made to examine the growth trends in area, production and yield of sugarcane in factory areas and also the trends in prices paid by the sugar factories to sugarcane growers in Marathwada during 1981-82 to 1997-98.

GROWTH OF SUGAR INDUSTRY IN INDIA AND MAHARASHTRA

Table 1 explains the growth of sugar industry in India from 1981-82 to 2003-04. During 1981-82, there were 320 sugar factories, which increased to 435 in 2003-04. Number of sugar factories in India showed increasing trend during the study period. Thereafter, sugar production declined to 106.09 lakh tonnes in 1992-93 and further to 98.33 lakh tonnes in 1993-94. But in the subsequent year it jumped to 185.37 lakh tonnes in 2001-02 and further to 210.46 lakh tonnes in 2002-03. In 2003-04, the sugar produced by the sugar factories came down to 135.46 lakh tonnes. On an average, the sugar production was 119.96 lakh tonnes per year. The annual average growth rate of sugar production was 0.52 per cent.

During the study period, on an average, the recovery percentage of sugar in India was about 10 per cent. The average recovery was 10.03 per cent. The annual average growth rate of sugar recovery was 0.08 per cent. During 1981-82, the area under sugarcane was 31.93 lakh hectares, which went up to 39.95 lakh hectares in 2003-04. During the twenty three years period, on an average, the area under sugarcane was 36.75 lakh hectares per year. The area under sugarcane was lowest in 1985-86 (i.e. 28.50 lakh hectares) due to drought conditions and it was the highest in 2001-02 (i.e. 44.30 lakh hectares) due to favourable weather conditions. The average annual growth rate of sugarcane area was 0.17 per cent.

Table 1
Growth of Sugar Industry in India During 1981-82 to 2003-04

Year	*Area under sugarcane (lakh hectares)*	*Sugarcane production (lakh metric tonnes)*	*Yield (tonnes/ ha.)*	*Sugarcane crushed (lakh metric tonnes)*	*Sugar production (lakh metric tonnes)*	*Average sugar recovery (per cent)*
1981-82	31.93	1864	54.8	540.10	54.60	9.66
1982-83	33.58	1895	56.4	570.15	54.80	9.95
1983-84	31.10	1741	56.0	590.24	59.17	10.02
1984-85	29.53	1703	57.7	600.90	61.48	10.22
1985-86	28.50	1706	59.9	685.66	70.16	10.23
1986-87	30.79	1861	60.4	852.02	85.02	9.98
1987-88	32.79	1967	60.0	939.36	90.10	9.70
1988-89	33.29	2030	61.0	856.47	87.53	10.22
1989-90	34.05	2226	65.4	1111.58	109.90	9.89
1990-91	36.86	2410	66.1	1223.38	124.70	9.84
1991-92	38.44	2539	63.8	1339.50	134.05	10.01
1992-93	35.72	2280	67.1	1030.08	106.09	10.30
1993-94	34.22	2296	71.1	983.38	98.33	10.00
1994-95	38.15	2712	69.9	1474.30	146.43	9.92
1995-96	41.47	2828	67.8	1747.26	164.43	9.90
1996-97	41.74	2776	66.5	1303.79	129.05	9.90
1997-98	39.40	2795	71.1	1291.35	128.52	9.95
1998-99	40.55	2887	71.2	1575.61	155.39	9.86
1999-00	42.20	2993	70.9	1784.94	182.00	10.20
2000-01	43.16	2960	68.6	1766.60	185.11	10.48

Contd...

Table 1 contd.

Year	*Area under sugarcane (lakh hectares)*	*Sugarcane production (lakh metric tonnes)*	*Yield (tonnes/ ha.)*	*Sugarcane crushed (lakh metric tonnes)*	*Sugar production (lakh metric tonnes)*	*Average sugar recovery per cent*
2001-02	44.30	2984	67.4	1803.86	185.37	10.27
2002-03	43.61	6816	64.6	1943.65	210.46	10.36
2003-04	39.95	2362	59.1	1325.11	135.46	10.22
Average	36.75	2375	64.21	1188.66	119.96	10.03
Annual Simple Growth Rate (%)	0.17	0.19	0.09	0.33	0.52	0.08

Source: Cooperative Sugar, August 2004.

The average sugarcane yield in India showed increasing trend during the period under study. During 1981-82 the yield of sugarcane was 54.8 tonnes per hectare, which increased and reached up to 59.1 tonnes per hectare in 2003-04. On an average, the yield of sugarcane was 64.21 tonnes per hectare during the study period. The annual average growth rate of yield of sugarcane was 0.09 per cent. The sugarcane yield showed year to year fluctuations with almost negligible growth during this period. The sugarcane production in India showed a positive trend during the study period. During 1981-82 the sugarcane production in India was 1864 lakh tonnes, which increased up to 2362 lakh tonnes in 2003-04. On an average, the sugarcane production was 2375 lakh tonnes per year during the study period. The annual average growth rate of sugarcane production was 0.19 per cent. During 1981-82 sugarcane crushed in India was 540.10 lakh metric tonnes, which increased up to 1325.11 lakh metric tonnes in 2002-03, the sugarcane crushed showed increasing trend during the study period. On an average, the sugarcane crushed was 1188.66 lakh tonnes per year during the study period. The annual average growth rate of sugarcane crushed was 0.33 per cent.

Table 2 explains the growth of sugar industry in Maharashtra during 1981-82 to 2003-04. During 1981-82,

Table 2
Growth of Sugar Industry in Maharashtra During 1981-82 to 2003-04

Year	*Area under sugarcane (lakh hectares)*	*Sugarcane production (lakh metric tonnes)*	*Yield (tonnes / ha.)*	*Sugarcane crushed (lakh metric tonnes)*	*Sugar production (lakh metric tonnes)*	*Average sugar recovery (per cent)*
1981-82	2.97	288	96.9	244.88	30.26	10.70
1982-83	3.26	313	96.3	238.20	30.25	10.95
1983-84	2.94	265	90.3	158.17	19.93	11.13
1984-85	1.92	263	90.1	185.60	23.11	11.08
1985-86	2.65	237	89.4	190.21	23.88	11.20
1986-87	2.80	241	86.1	197.77	25.39	10.98
1987-88	2.92	250	85.6	245.31	27.95	10.83
1988-89	3.14	255	81.1	238.15	26.29	11.04
1989-90	3.83	340	88.8	366.29	39.21	10.71
1990-91	4.44	384	86.5	383.44	41.19	10.89
1991-92	5.18	361	79.8	376.57	42.13	11.19
1992-93	5.80	308	76.4	297.36	33.60	11.30
1993-94	5.80	278	81.1	246.85	27.46	11.13
1994-95	5.13	442	85.5	459.97	50.25	10.92
1995-96	5.80	467	80.4	514.58	53.94	10.49
1996-97	5.16	418	81.0	310.13	34.45	11.11
1997-98	4.60	382	83.0	345.77	38.47	11.13
1998-99	5.30	472	89.0	479.00	53.37	11.16
1999-00	5.90	531	90.1	570.95	65.03	11.40
2000-01	5.95	496	83.3	676.49	67.05	11.64
2001-02	5.78	451	78.1	483.87	56.12	11.62
2002-03	5.99	370	61.80	534.74	62.21	11.68
2003-04	5.26	270	51.30	290.39	31.71	10.94
Average	4.46	351	83.13	339.33	39.27	11.10
Annual Simple Growth Rate (%)	0.28	-0.90	-0.78	0.81	-0.97	0.01

Sources: 1. The Report of the Committee for Recommending a Package for Rehabilitation of Sick Sugar Factories in Cooperative Sector published by Government of Maharashtra, Bombay, June 1999.
2. Cooperative Sugar, August 2004.

there were only 78 sugar factories in the State which increased to 90 in 1989-90 and further to 136 in 2003-04. The number of sugar factories increased works out at 18 and 9 during the eighties and nineties respectively in Maharashtra State. In 1981-82 all these sugar factories have produced 30.26 lakh metric tonnes of sugar which increased to 65.03 lakh metric tonnes in 1999-00 and 67.05 metric tonnes in 2000-01, but thereafter showed sharp decline due to drought years. On an average, 39.27 metric tonnes of sugar per year have been produced by the sugar factories in Maharashtra during 1981 to 2003. The annual average growth rate of sugar production was –0.97 per cent.

During the study period, the average sugar recovery in Maharashtra was 11.10 per cent, it was around 10 per cent in India. The annual average growth rate of sugar recovery was 0.01 per cent.

With the increase in number of sugar factories, the area under sugarcane has also increased in Maharashtra. In 1981-82, it was 2.97 lakh hectares which showed ups and downs in the subsequent years and reached to 5.99 lakh hectares in 2002-03. During the eighties, the sugarcane acreage in the factory areas in Maharashtra was as low as 1.92 lakh hectares in 1984-85 and as high as 3.83 lakh hectares in 1989-90. During the nineties the acreage under sugarcane in factory areas of Maharashtra showed a continuously rising trend, with the exception in the year 1995-96, and reached to a level of 5.90 lakh hectares in 1999-2000. During the study period, the annual average growth rate of area under sugarcane was 0.28 per cent.

The sugarcane production in the factory areas of Maharashtra showed a mixed trend during the period under study. It was 288 lakh tonnes in 1981-82 which went up to 467 lakh tonnes in 1995-96 and further to 531 lakh tonnes in 1999-2000. The ups and downs in sugarcane production can be attributed to weather and rainfall conditions existed in different years. The annual average growth rate of sugarcane production was –0.36 per cent.

The yield of sugarcane showed a clear-cut decreasing trend till 1988-89. It was 96.9 tonnes per hectare in 1981-82 and decreased continuously to 81.8 tonnes per hectare in 1988-89. Afterwards it showed ups and downs and reached to 90.1 tonnes per hectare in 1999-2000. During the whole period under consideration, the yield of sugarcane in the factory areas of Maharashtra remained at 83.13 tonnes per hectare. The annual average growth rate of sugarcane yield was –0.78 per cent.

CAPACITY UTILIZATION

Table 3 reveals that Marathwada region has registered the lowest percentage of utilization of plant capacity as compared to south and central zone as well as at state level. South zone has recorded highest percentage of utilization of plant capacity i.e. 99 per cent, followed by central zone i.e. 96 per cent. But the under utilization of plant capacity in Marathwada, on an average, was 21 per cent. If the same is compared to south and central zones it was less by 20 per cent and 17 percentage point respectively.

Table 3
Zone-wise Percentage Utilization of Plant Capacity in Maharashtra

Year	*Marathwada*	*South zone*	*Central zone*	*Maharashtra state*
1996-97	66.37	98.09	95.24	85.83
1997-98	71.54	95.99	95.29	87.31
1998-99	77.80	98.88	94.14	90.24
1999-00	82.88	100.46	97.25	90.86
2000-01	94.74	104.05	103.77	99.36
Average per cent	79.00	99.00	96.00	91.00

Source: Performance of Sugar Factories in Maharashtra, Vasantdada Sugar Institute, Pune, 2003-04.

GROWTH OF SUGAR INDUSTRY IN MARATHWADA

With the help of available data, keeping in mind the sugar industry of Maharashtra, the position of sugar factories in Marathwada region is presented in table 4.

In 1981-82 there were 15 sugar factories in operation in Marathwada region, which increased to 22 in 1990-91. Seven sugar factories were newly set up in the decade 1981

Table 4
Growth of Sugar Industry in Marathwada During 1981-82 to 1996-97

Year	*Area under sugarcane (thousand hectares)*	*Sugarcane production (lakh tonnes)*	*Yield (tonnes / ha.)*	*Number of sugar factories*	*Duration of crushing season (days)*
1981-82	58.6	43.43	74.11	15	210
1982-83	73.5	60.58	82.42	16	190
1983-84	53.7	35.48	66.07	17	87
1984-85	61.6	41.1	66.72	18	130
1985-86	50.9	33.3	65.42	21	112
1986-87	48.8	30.29	62.06	22	98
1987-88	53.6	41.61	77.68	22	169
1988-89	78.3	45.02	57.49	23	137
1989-90	96.2	75.77	78.76	26	224
1990-91	117.7	76.6	65.18	29	219
1991-92	123.8	78.18	63.15	31	190
1992-93	94.8	61.04	64.39	31	131
1993-94	80.0	56.13	70.17	31	123
1994-95	137.4	103.08	75.02	32	226
1995-96	80.0	94.25	66.28	32	214
1996-97	105.1	68.90	84.2	32	138
Average	82.24	58.85	72.01	20	162.37
Annual Simple Growth Rate (%)	7.98	8.68	4.38		6.57

Table 4. Contd...

Year	*Sugarcane crushed (lakh tonnes)*	*Sugar production (lakh tonnes)*	*Average sugar recovery (per cent)*	*Capacity utilization (per cent)*
1981-82	38.63	3.67	9.54	123.72
1982-83	37.19	3.83	10.21	114.46
1983-84	15.33	1.60	10.2	46.44
1984-85	28.89	3.03	10.31	88.46
1985-86	24.14	2.50	9.6	64.48
1986-87	19.58	2.01	9.54	55.42
1987-88	29.29	2.86	9.74	80.72
1988-89	36.13	3.65	10.25	101.45
1989-90	64.07	5.40	10.15	107.96

Table 4. Contd...

Year	*Sugarcane crushed (lakh tonnes)*	*Sugar production (lakh tonnes)*	*Average sugar recovery (per cent)*	*Capacity utilization (per cent)*
1990-91	68.10	7.10	10.43	95.00
1991-92	59.50	6.41	10.69	93.73
1992-93	31.81	3.38	10.50	80.99
1993-94	28.35	2.91	9.94	79.60
1994-95	71.01	7.16	9.97	87.69
1995-96	64.11	6.26	9.59	80.09
1996-97	31.11	3.42	10.12	81.66
Average	40.45	3.62	10.04	86.36
Annual Simple Growth Rate (%)	11.18	13.84	0.46	2.33

Source: Annual Reports of all Sugar Factories in the Marathwada Region, 1981-82 to 1996-97.

to 1991. In 1997-98 there were 30 sugar factories in Marathwada region and all of them were established in cooperative sector. These sugar factories had covered the sugarcane area to the tune of 58.6 thousand hectares in 1981-82 which increased to 105.10 thousand hectares in 1996-97. The area under sugarcane in the factory areas of Marathwada was as high as 137.4 thousand hectares in 1994-95 and as low as 48.8 in 1986-87. Large year to year variations are observed in the sugarcane area within operational area of sugar factories in Marathwada during the period under consideration. The per year average area under sugarcane in the factory areas of Marathwada was 82.24 thousand hectares. The annual average growth rate of sugarcane area was 7.98 per cent.

The sugarcane production in Marathwada showed a mixed trend during the study period. During 1981-82, sugarcane production in Marathwada was 43.43 lakh metric tonnes which increased to 68.90 lakh metric tonnes in 1996-97. The per year average sugarcane production in the factory areas of Marathwada was 58.85 tonnes. The annual average growth rate of sugarcane production was 8.68 per cent.

The average sugarcane yield also showed mixed trend during the study period. The average sugarcane yield in the factory areas was 74.11 metric tonnes per hectare in 1981-82, which increased and reached up to 84.2 metric tonnes per hectare in 1996-97. The average sugarcane yield in the factory areas was the highest in 1996-97 (i.e. 84.2 metric tonnes) per hectare and it was the lowest (i.e. 62.06 metric tonnes per hectare) in 1986-87. On an average, the sugarcane yield was 72.01 metric tonnes during the study period. The annual average growth rate of yield of sugarcane was 4.38 per cent.

The sugarcane crushed in the factory areas of Marathwada showed a mixed trend during the eighties and nineties. It was 38.63 lakh tonnes in 1981-82 which went down to 31.11 lakh tonnes in 1996-97. On an average, the sugarcane crushed in Marathwada was 40.45 lakh tonnes during the study period. The annual average growth rate of sugarcane crushed was 11.18 per cent. The sugar production in the factory areas of Marathwada was 3.67 lakh tonnes in 1981-82 which went down to 3.42 lakh tonnes in 1996-97. The sugar production in the factory areas of Marathwada was as high as 7.16 lakh tonnes in 1994-95 and as low as 1.60 lakh tonnes in 1983-84. On an average, the sugar production was 3.62 lakh tonnes during the study period. The annual average growth rate of sugar production was 13.84 per cent.

During the study period, the average recovery percentage of sugar in Marathwada was 10.04 per cent. The annual average growth rate of average recovery of sugar was 0.46 per cent. The capacity utilization by the sugar factories in Marathwada during the study period was 86.36 per cent. The annual average growth rate in their capacity utilization was 2.33 per cent.

DISTRICTWISE NUMBER OF SUGAR FACTORIES IN THE MARATHWADA REGION

No industrial or agricultural development could take place in this region as long as it was under the regime of Nizam's State. When this region was attached to Maharashtra State, the Government of Maharashtra paid attention towards agricultural and industrial development of this region.

The data presented in table 5 throws light on the districtwise number of sugar factories alongwith their crushing capacity in the Marathwada region. There was only one privately owned sugar factory of M/s Dhoot and Co., which was established in 1957 at Gangapur. Thereafter, this sugar factory was cooperativised in 1968. This was the first cooperative sugar factory in the Marathwada region. When this sugar factory was successfully cooperativised, some new cooperative sugar factories came into existence in 1969.

Table 5
Districtwise Number of Sugar Factories in Marathwada.

Sr. No.	*Name of sugar factory*	*Newly licensed sugar factory*	*Daily tonnes crushing capacity (TCD)*	*Year of establish-ment*	*Previous daily tonnes crushing capacity (TCD)*
	Aurangabad District	1			
1.	Gangapur S.S.K. Ltd., Gangapur		2000	1968	Before 1990 TCD was 1016
2.	Kannad S.S.K. Ltd., Kannad		1250	1969	1250
3.	Sant Eknath S.S.K. Ltd., Paithan		1250	1969	1250
4.	Siddheshwar S.S.K. Ltd., Sillod		2000	1969	Before 1990 TCD was 1250
5.	Vinayak S.S.K. Ltd., Vaijapur		2500	1969	Before 1994 TCD was 1250
	Jalna District				
6.	Samarth S.S.K. Ltd., Wadigodri, Ambad		2500	1982	Before 1994 TCD was 1250
7.	Jalna S.S.K. Ltd., Ramnagar, Jalna		1250	1984	1250
	Beed District	2			
8.	Ambajogai S.S.K. Ltd., Ambajogai		2500	1969	Before 1991 TCD was 1250
9.	Jaibhavani S.S.K. Ltd., Georai		2500	1973	Before 1990 TCD was 1250

Contd...

Table 5. Contd...

Sr. No.	*Name of sugar factory*	*Newly licensed sugar factory*	*Daily tonnes crushing capacity (TCD)*	*Year of establishment*	*Previous daily tonnes crushing capacity (TCD)*
10.	Kada S.S.K. Ltd., Ashti		1250	1974	1250
11.	Gajanan S.S.K. Ltd., Navgan Rajuri		1250	1982	1250
	Parbhani District	2			
12.	Godavari Dudhana S.S.K. Ltd.		1250	1975	1250
13.	Marathwada S.S.K. Ltd., Kalamnuri		1250	1969	1250
14.	Purna S.S.K. Ltd., Basmatnagar, Basmat		2500	1973	Before 1990 TCD was 1250
	Nanded District	3			
15.	Kalambar Vibhag S.S.K. Ltd., Kandhar		1250	1966	1250
16.	Godavari Manar S.S.K. Ltd., Shankarnagar, Biloli		2500	1979	Before 1992 TCD was 1250
17.	Shankar S.S.K. Ltd., Kusumnagar Bhokar		1250	1984	1250
	Osmanabad District	1			1250
18.	Terna S.S.K. Ltd., Dhoki		3500	1965	Before 1990 TCD was 2000
19.	Tuljabhavani S.S.K. Ltd., Naldurg		1250	1983	1250
	Latur District	2			
20.	Shetkari S.S.K. Ltd., Killari		1250	1969	1250
21.	Jai Jawan Jai Kisan S.S.K. Ltd., Nalegaon		1250	1982	1250
22.	Manjra S.S.K. Ltd., Latur		1250	1984	1250
	Marathwada	12	38750		

Note: The crushing capacity of all newly licensed sugar factories is 2500 TCD each.

Sources: 1. Report of the Maharashtra Rajya Sahakari Sakhar Karkhana Sangh Ltd., Mumbai, Regional Office, Aurangabad, February, 2000.

2. Director of Sugar, Maharashtra State, Pune.

At present, 5 sugar factories are working in the Aurangabad district. They are Gangapur S.S.K. Ltd., Gangapur; Kannad S.S.K. Ltd., Kannad; Sant Eknath S.S.K. Ltd., Paithan; Siddheshwar S.S.K. Ltd., Sillod; and Vinayak S.S.K. Ltd., Vaijapur. The crushing capacity of Gangapur S.S.K. Ltd. was 1016 daily tonnes crushing capacity (TCD) which increased to 2000 TCD in 1989-90. Recently the factory has also started distillery plant. The Siddheshwar S.S.K. Ltd., Sillod has also increased its crushing capacity to 2000 TCD in 1989-90. The Vinayak S.S.K. Ltd., Vaijapur has also increased its crushing capacity to 2500 TCD in 1993-94. The crushing capacity of the remaining 2 sugar factories is 1250 TCD each. In addition to these, one more cooperative sugar factory has started at Fulambri in Aurangabad district (i.e. Deogiri S.S.K. Ltd.). The crushing capacity of the newly licensed sugar factory will be 2500 TCD as per the revised norms of central government.

Two sugar factories are operating in Jalna district. The crushing capacity of Samarth S.S.K. Ltd., Wadigodri was initially 1250 TCD which increased to 2500 TCD in 1993-94. The crushing capacity of Jalna S.S.K. Ltd., Ramnagar, is 1250 TCD. In addition to these, one more cooperative sugar factory is very recently started at Partur (i.e. Bageshwari S.S.K. Ltd.) in Jalna district.

At present there are 4 sugar factories in Beed district. The crushing capacity of these sugar factories is 1250 TCD each, but in the case of Jaibhavani S.S.K. Ltd., Georai, the crushing capacity has increased to 2500 TCD in 1990. The crushing capacity of Ambajogai S.S.K. Ltd., Ambajogai was initially 1250 TCD which increased to 2500 TCD in 1991. In addition to these 2 more sugar factories are newly licensed and they have started working viz. at Manjlegaon and Parli-Vaijanath. The work of erection of one more sugar factory near Kaij (i.e. Padmashri Vikhe Patil S.S.K. Ltd.) is in progress.

In Parbhani district, 3 sugar factories are working at present having the crushing capacity of 1250 TCD each, but in the case of Purna S.S.K. Ltd., Basmat, the crushing capacity has increased to 2500 TCD in 1990. Two more new sugar factories are coming up in this district.

In Nanded district, 3 sugar factories are working at present having the crushing capacity of 1250 TCD each. But in the case of Godavari Manar S.S.K. Ltd., Biloli, the crushing capacity has increased to 2500 TCD in 1992. Licenses are sanctioned to 3 more sugar factories in this district.

In Osmanabad district there are only two sugar factories and one more sugar factory is newly licensed. The more important point to be noted here is that the Terna S.S.K. Ltd., Dhoki, has increased its crushing capacity up to 3500 TCD in 1989-90. Another factory is located in Tuljapur taluka viz., Tuljabhavani S.S.K. Ltd., Naldurg.

In Latur district 3 sugar factories are working and two more sugar factories are granted licenses. The crushing capacity of each existing sugar factory is 1250 TCD.

Thus, there are 22 cooperative sugar factories in operation and 10 new sugar factories are coming up in Marathwada region. It means that within three to four years 35 sugar factories will be in operation in this region.

This shows that the sugar industry is developing at a faster rate in this region. Among the 8 districts of Marathwada, large number of sugar factories are located in Aurangabad district and very few are located in Osmanabad and Jalna districts. The second important point is that these sugar factories are trying to establish by-product units such as distillery and paper plants from their waste products. This may lead to increased employment opportunity, and an increase in the income of the farmers in this region.

CAPACITY UTILIZATION OF SUGAR FACTORIES IN MARATHWADA

To measure the economic development of sugar industry in a region, we selected capacity utilization as an indicator. It was felt that total number of factories in a region or total installed capacity in a region will not quite to give us the correct picture of economic development in that region. If the number of factories is very large and the average installed capacity is low, it will not give us the correct picture. Similarly, if we choose installed capacity as a measure, then also we may obtain misleading conclusion because the installed capacity may not be utilized fully. Full capacity utilization is very important for the proper and economically sound working of a sugar factory. To achieve this, installed capacity should be in tune with the sugarcane supply. Barring the drought years, the sugar factory should be able to utilize its production capacity fully.

The financial condition of a sugar factory depends upon its capacity utilization. According to the norms determined by the experts, for hundred per cent capacity utilization, a sugar factory must get adequate quantity of sugarcane for 180 days in a crushing season. The formula being used to work out the required quantity of sugarcane is as follows:

100 per cent capacity utilization of a sugar factory = 180 net crushing days x crushing capacity

For example, if crushing capacity of a sugar factory is 1250 TCD then for its 100 per cent capacity utilization, the sugar factory must get sugarcane for net 180 crushing days, that is, 180 x 1250 = 2,25,000 metric tonnes during a season.

TRENDS IN CRUSHING DAYS OF SUGAR FACTORIES IN MARATHWADA

The total crushing of sugarcane by a sugar factory depends on its working days in a crushing season and the gross rate of crushing per day. Higher the gross rate of crushing per day and the longest is the season, the maximum is going to be the crushing of sugarcane by the sugar factory, reflected in maximum capacity utilization of the factory. The longest crushing season cannot be considered at the best at the cost of the loss of recovery of sugar. The sugarcane crop matures during October/ November and the sucrose contents in the crop are maximum till the end of April. Thereafter, due to hot weather, the sugar content in the sugarcane crop starts decreasing. Thus from middle of October to end of April 196 days are available of which 26 days (2 days at the end of every fortnight) are required for cleaning of machinery. The sugar factory can, therefore, get 170 days for undertaking crushing and during this period the highest possible rate of crushing per day has to be achieved. Though the crushing season of 160 days is considered optimum, it is possible to have the crushing season of at least 170 days without affecting the recovery of sugar in Maharashtra.

As per the State Government norms, a sugar factory should get adequate supply of sugarcane at least for 160 days for 100 per cent capacity utilization in the Maharashtra state, and as per the national norms it must get adequate quantity of sugarcane for 180 days for 100 per cent capacity utilization. Generally, a crushing season starts during the third week of November and ends by the end of April.

Table 6 shows data about the total number of crushing days during a crushing season in Marathwada during 1981-82 to 1998-99. The total number of crushing days of sugar factories in Marathwada has shown a decreasing trend during the period 1981-82 to 1986-87 from 228 days to merely 95 days. Thereafter, the number of crushing days has shown a mixed trend. For the entire period under study, the average number of crushing days amounts to about 167 days, which is higher than the required 160 days for full utilization of crushing capacity of sugar factories in Marathwada. It is also important to note that the number of crushing days was more than 200 days in five years. Further, during eight years the crushing season of sugar factories exceeded 160 days.

Table 7 shows the data about districtwise crushing days of sugar factories in Marathwada during 1981-82 to 1998-99.

The district-wise picture reveals that the average number of crushing days for the whole period of eighteen years exceeded 160 days in case of all the districts in Marathwada except Parbhani district. For Parbhani district, it was 158.61 days. There are not very much inter-district differences with respect to mean number of crushing days over the entire period under study.

Table 6
Total Crushing Days of Sugar Factories in Marathwada During 1981-82 to 1998-99

Year	*Total crushing days*
1981-82	228
1982-83	193
1983-84	138
1984-85	127
1985-86	130
1986-87	95
1987-88	167
1988-89	142
1989-90	252
1990-91	237
1991-92	191
1992-93	131
1993-94	123
1994-95	226
1995-96	214
1996-97	138
1997-98	129
1998-99	143
Average	166.88

Sources: 1. Working Results of Sugar Factories in Maharashtra, Vasantdada Sugar Institute, Pune, 1981-82 to 1998-99.
2. Annual Reports of All Sugar Factories in Marathwada.

Table 7
Districtwise Total Crushing Days of Sugar Factories in Marathwada During 1981-82 to 1998-99

Year	*Auranga-bad*	*Jalna*	*Parbhani*	*Beed*	*Nanded*	*Osmana bad*	*Latur*
1981-82	233	-	185	231	223	276	232
1982-83	189	-	172	216	208	209	160
1983-84	121	-	128	170	185	110	112
1984-85	125	-	121	122	142	107	155
1985-86	114	116	119	142	124	154	140

Contd...

Table 7. Contd...

Year	*Aurangabad*	*Jalna*	*Parbhani*	*Beed*	*Nanded*	*Osmanabad*	*Latur*
1986-87	97	60	102	123	151	60	75
1987-88	179	169	171	169	176	160	158
1988-89	140	148	125	166	121	157	136
1989-90	256	243	256	274	235	249	245
1990-91	226	234	237	252	238	237	232
1991-92	196	200	203	167	202	172	196
1992-93	145	162	134	108	132	127	108
1993-94	148	133	104	100	131	103	144
1994-95	199	237	225	212	232	236	244
1995-96	209	224	207	209	220	219	212
1996-97	107	133	148	146	145	150	137
1997-98	108	72	126	153	118	183	140
1998-99	171	168	102	147	127	137	152
Average	164.61	164.21	158.61	172.61	173	169.22	165.78

Sources: 1. Working Results of Sugar Factories in Maharashtra, Vasantdada Sugar Institute, Pune, 1981-82 to 1998-99.
2. Annual Reports of All Sugar Factories in Marathwada.

PRICE OF SUGARCANE

The Bureau of Industrial Costs and Prices (BICP), instead of deriving actual cost of production in a particular year, depends upon the recently available data. Similarly, Statutory Minimum Price (SMP) is generally notional. In this regard, BICP says that there are unavoidable difficulties in the quantification of so called disparity. After considering the difficulties, S.N. Mane[8] on the basis of index given for the period 1982-83 to 1998-99, has tried to give some estimates.

From the table 8 it can be seen that there has been 100 per cent increase in statutory minimum price of sugarcane during 1982-83 to 1998-99 period. However, an increase in State Advised Price (SAP) was more than the 100 per cent. Particularly, though the statutory minimum price increased 100 per cent, the percentage of SAP to statutory minimum price, in that decade, was four times (400 per cent). It means, cross vertical disparity is big and more serious problem than the equi-vertical disparity. An interesting thing is that, recently the BICP has started to increase, without touching

SAP, the statutory minimum price in order to reduce the continuously increasing disparity, irrespective of either increase or decrease in the average sugar recovery. Thus, in actual practice, the sugar factories pay much higher cane price than the statutory minimum price on the advice of the state government.

Table 8
All India Sugarcane Yield and Statutory Minimum Price of Sugarcane During 1982-83 to 1998-99

Years	*Yield (Tonnes/ ha.)*	*SMP (RS/Qt.)*	*Linked to Basic Recovery*	*Premium on every 0.1 per cent increase in recovery*	*Range of minimum cane price on the basis of Cols. 3, 4 & 5*
1	2	3	4	5	6
1982-83	56.4	13.00	8.5	0.152941	13.00 to 19.22
1983-84	56.0	13.50	8.5	0.158824	13.00 to 26.20
1984-85	57.7	14.00	8.5	0.164706	14.00 to 20.42
1985-86	59.9	16.50	8.5	0.19412	16.50 to 24.07
1986-87	60.4	17.00	8.5	0.20	17.00 to 25.00
1987-88	60.0	18.50	8.5	0.21765	18.50 to 26.77
1988-89	61.0	19.50	8.5	0.2294	19.50 to 27.99
1989-90	65.6	22.00	8.5	0.2588	22.00 to 32.09
1990-91	65.4	23.00	8.5	0.270588	23.00 to 34.36
1991-92	66.1	26.00	8.5	0.305882	26.00 to 38.54
1992-93	63.8	31.00	8.5	0.364706	31.00 to 47.41
1993-94	67.1	34.50	8.5	0.405882	34.50 to 53.17
1994-95	71.1	39.10	8.5	0.46	38.10 to 66.40
1995-96	68.4	42.50	8.5	0.54	39.10 to 66.40
1996-97	66.9	45.90	8.5	0.57	39.10 to 66.40
1997-98	67.5	48.50	8.5	0.60	39.10 to 66.40
1998-99	60.2	52.70	8.5	0.62	39.10 to 66.40

Sources: 1. Mane S.N., Presidential Address, "Sugarcane Price Policy in India" Marathi Arthashastra Parishad, 19th Annual Conference, Tilak Maharashtra University, Pune, 1995.
2. Co-operative Sugar, August, 1999.

Table 9 indicates the price of sugarcane declared by the Government of India, and price recommended by the State Government from 1981-82 to 1999-2000.

Table 9
Price of Sugarcane Recommended by the State and Central Governments During 1981-82 to 1999-2000

(Rs./tonne)

Year	*Price recommended by State Government*	*Price declared by Central Government*
1981-82	188.00	130.00
1982-83	191.20	130.00
1983-84	196.90	135.00
1984-85	204.20	140.00
1985-86	240.70	165.00
1986-87	250.00	170.00
1987-88	267.70	185.00
1988-89	279.90	195.00
1989-90	320.90	230.00
1990-91	343.60	230.00
1991-92	260.00	260.00
1992-93	290.00	310.00
1993-94	365.00	345.00
1994-95	425.00	391.00
1995-96	450.00	425.00
1996-97	460.00	459.00
1997-98	540.00	484.50
1998-99	540.00	527.00
1999-2000	560.00	561.00
Average	335.43	288.03

Source: Various Issues of Annual Report of Maharashtra Rajya Sahakari Sakhar Karkhana Sangh Ltd., Mumbai.

This table shows that the price recommended by the State Government in 1981-82 was only Rs. 188 per metric tonne and the price declared by Central Government was Rs. 130 per metric tonne. That means it was Rs.188.00 and Rs. 130.00 per quintal respectively during the year 1981-82. Table 9 shows that there has been continuous rise in price declared by state and central governments during 1981-82 to 1999-2000. In the decade 1981-82 to 1990-91 price recommended by State Government was increased by 82.76 per cent (from Rs. 188 per metric tonne to Rs. 343.60 per metric tonne). In 1991-92 it was decreased up to Rs. 260 per metric tonne in comparison to price in previous year. After 1991-92 the price fixed by State Government showed a rising trend, it was Rs. 260 per tonne in 1991-92 which increased and reached up to Rs. 560 per tonne in 1999-2000. The increase was 115 per cent in this period. On an average, the sugarcane price fixed by State Government was Rs. 335.43 per metric tonne during the study period. As well as the price fixed by the Central Government shows continuously rising trend during the study period. During the study period the price of sugarcane fixed by the Central Government was, on an average, Rs. 288.03 per metric tonne. In 1981-82 the price fixed by Central Government was Rs. 130 per metric tonne which increased and reached up to Rs. 561 per metric tonne in 1999-2000, the increase was 3.31 times. The price fixed by central and state governments showed a positive trend during the period from 1981-82 to 1999-2000.

SUGARCANE PRICES PAID BY SUGAR FACTORIES IN MARATHWADA

It is the fact that financial position of any sugar factory depends mainly upon two things: capacity utilization and recovery of sugar. If capacity utilization and recovery are maximum, the sugar factory can pay higher price to the cane growers. Some times sugar factories have to pay a more price to cane growers to attract adequate quantity of sugarcane with a view to utilize crushing capacity to the maximum extent.

Table 10 shows the districtwise price paid for sugarcane by the sugar factories in Marathwada region during 1981-82 to 1997-98. The data presented in table 10 reveals that statutory minimum price of sugarcane fixed by the state government has been higher than the price declared by the central government during most of the years under study. Further, there has been upward revision in the price of sugarcane declared by both central and state government during the period under study. It is mandatory for the sugar factories to pay at least the statutory minimum price fixed by central and state governments. Therefore, data shown in

Table 10
Price Paid for Sugarcane by Sugar Factories in Marathwada During 1981-82 to 1997-98

(Rs./tonne)

Year	*Aurangabad*	*Jalna*	*Beed*	*Parbhani*	*Nanded*	*Osmanabad*	*Latur*
1981-82	180	-	180	180	180	184	180
1982-83	170	-	157	154	150	187	182
1983-84	159	-	257	150	150	150	170
1984-85	235	207	219	178	181	258	235
1985-86	240	243	251	238	220	270	236
1986-87	244	257	250	243	233	259	239
1987-88	268	269	258	258	240	283	258
1988-89	270	297	278	267	242	331	289
1989-90	327	352	307	288	312	309	349
1990-91	344	389	309	291	350	325	400
1991-92	345	415	315	285	427	340	420
1992-93	429	446	335	327	482	350	445
1993-94	706	629	590	367	595	435	656
1994-95	632	617	570	417	581	525	669
1995-96	502	528	460	493	477	564	727
1996-97	508	610	473	485	477	589	784
1997-98	540	604	673	525	540	610	823
Average	359	419	346	303	417	352	415

Source: Annual Reports of All Sugar Factories in Marathwada, 1981-82 to 1997-98.

table 10 indicates that all the sugar factories in Marathwada have paid the price for cane crop higher than what has been recommended by the government for the respective years. In case of Aurangabad district, the price paid for sugarcane was Rs. 180 per tonne in 1981-82 and Rs. 540 per tonne in 1997-98. On an average, the price paid by the sugar factories in Aurangabad district was Rs. 359 per tonne per year. Among the six districts the sugar factories of Jalna district have paid the highest sugarcane price and factories in Nanded and Latur districts lie at the bottom in this respect.

References

1. Noel Deer, History of Sugar, Vol. I, Chapman and Hall Ltd., London, 1949.

2. Kalyankar, S.P., Kosle P.V. and Nagargoje S.R., Contribution of Yield and Area to Increase Sugarcane Production in Maharashtra and India, Maharashtra Journal of Agricultural Economics, Vol. 7, No. 1, March, 1995.
3. Koranne V.M., Nagapure S.C. and Ulemale D.H., Growth Performance of Sugarcane in Maharashtra State, Maharashtra Journal of Agricultural Economics, Vol. 7, No. 1, March, 1995.
4. Singhal Vikas, Handbook of Indian Agriculture, Vikas Publishing House Private Limited, New Delhi, 1995.
5. Chief Statistician, Commissionerate of Agriculture, Pune. The Districtwise Area, Production and Productivity of Principal Crops in Maharashtra State, 1994-95 to 1995-96.
6. Koranne V.M., Nagapure S.C. and Ulemale D.H., op cit.
7. Baviskar B.S., Indian Sugar : Powers to the Peasants, Cooperative Sugar, April, 1999.
8. Mane S.N., Sugarcane Price Policy in India, Presidential Address, Marathi Arthashastra Parishad, 19th Annual Conference, Tilak Maharashtra University, Pune, 1995.

5

Growth Trends in Sugarcane Crushed, Sugar Output and Sugar Recovery

Sugarcane is one of the important cash crops grown in India. Maharashtra is one of the major sugarcane and sugar producing states in India. Importance of sugarcane as a commercial crop has grown considerably during the last two decades in the country and particularly in the Maharashtra State. The Maharashtra State occupied a place of pride on the map of sugarcane of the country. Maharashtra State possesses about 19 per cent of the total sugarcane area of India and produces 20 per cent of sugarcane production and 38 per cent of sugar production at national level[1]. Thus, Maharashtra is one of the leading sugarcane growing states in India.

Geographically, the sugarcane cultivation is carried out under two distinct belts based on agro-climatic conditions, namely, the tropical belt and sub-tropical belt. The sugarcane crop is more suited to tropical conditions. Also, sugar recovery is better in areas having bright sunshine, dry and cool climate during its ripening period.

The important cane growing states of the tropical belt are Maharashtra, Karnataka, Andhra Pradesh, Tamil Nadu,

Gujarat and Orissa. The temperature variation in the tropical belt is on an average 10°C to 12°C but it never drops to 5°C. Under these conditions the cane growth and accumulation of sugar continue for longer period accounting for higher yield and recovery in these states[2]. However, between these states located in the tropical belt yield recovery varies considerably due to difference in temperature, humidity, soil type, irrigation etc.

The sub-tropical belt consists of important cane growing states of Uttar Pradesh, Bihar, Haryana and Punjab. The climate in these areas differs considerably from that in the tropical belt. The temperatures in these regions are extremely hot in summer and very cold in winters. The cold temperatures have a deteriorating effect on the growth of the cane crop and recovery of sugar. Sugarcane is grown in different states under varied conditions. Therefore, the quality of sugarcane varies in different regions. This is also reflected in recovery percentage of sugar obtained from cane.

The agro-climatic condition in Maharashtra, cultivation practices, use of fertilizers etc. are the factors responsible for the higher recovery of sugar in Maharashtra. The sugar recovery is affected by the tropical and subtropical conditions in the country. Thus, again in Uttar Pradesh, the largest producer, the recovery of sugar is comparatively low i.e. approximately 9.5 per cent. Similarly in the states of Bihar, Haryana, Rajasthan and West Bengal the recovery of sugar was lower than the all India average recovery of sugar. Maharashtra and Gujarat show a very high recovery percentage, followed by Karnataka, Tamil Nadu and Uttar Pradesh. Maharashtra and Gujarat achieved a recovery of sugar around 11 per cent, whereas Karnataka and Tamil Nadu have shown a recovery percentage of sugar around 10 per cent.

The percentage recovery of sugar depends on the quality of sugarcane as well as techniques of sugar production. Another important factor affecting the sugar recovery percentage is the time factor. Sugarcane is a weight losing raw material. If time is lost between the cutting and crushing a cane, the recovery percentage goes down. Therefore, the cane should reach the factory as far as possible.

In this chapter an attempt is made to analyse the growth trends in the sugarcane crushed, sugar output and sugar recovery in Marathwada during the period 1981-82 to 1998-99.

GROWTH TRENDS IN SUGARCANE CRUSHED

Table 1 shows the quantity of cane crushed by sugar factories in Marathwada region from 1981-82 to 1998-99. If we look at the table 1 it is seen that there are huge fluctuations in the quantity of cane crushed in Marathwada during the study period. The quantity of cane crushed varied between 15.33 lakh metric tonnes in 1983-84 to 71.01 lakh metric tonnes in 1994-95. In 1981-82 the quantity of cane crushed in Marathwada was 38.90 lakh metric tonnes which increased and reached up to 50.42 metric tonnes in 1998-99. Over the entire period, the quantity of cane crushed in Marathwada amounted to 40.47 lakh metric tonnes per year. The quantity of cane crushed in Marathwada was the highest in 1994-95 i.e. 71.01 lakh metric tonnes. This may be due to the confidence of growing more sugarcane amongst the farmers and provision of lift irrigation schemes to the farmers. And the lowest quantity of cane crushed was 15.73 lakh metric tonnes in 1983-84 due to lower production of sugarcane and less area under sugarcane due to drought conditions. The simple annual growth rate of cane crushed by the sugar factories in Marathwada was 12.89 per cent during the study period.

Table 2 shows the districtwise quantity of cane crushed by the sugar factories in Marathwada region during 1981-82 to 1998-99. This table indicates the huge fluctuation in cane crushed over the period in all the districts of Marathwada. In case of Aurangabad district, the quantity of cane crushed was 13.67 lakh metric tonnes in 1981-82 and 10.57 lakh metric tonnes in 1998-99. On an average, the cane crushed by the sugar factories in this district was 9.98 lakh metric tonnes

Table 1
Sugarcane Crushed in Marathwada During 1981-82 to 1998-99

Year	*Sugarcane crushed (Metric tonnes)*
1981-82	38.90
1982-83	34.20
1983-84	15.33
1984-85	28.92
1985-86	24.14
1986-87	19.62
1987-88	29.12
1988-89	36.13
1989-90	64.44
1990-91	66.99
1991-92	59.50
1992-93	31.81
1993-94	28.35
1994-95	71.01
1995-96	64.31
1996-97	31.11
1997-98	34.24
1998-99	50.42
Average	40.47
Simple annual growth rate (%)	12.89

Sources: 1. Working Results of Sugar Factories in Maharashtra, Vasantdada Sugar Institute, Pune, 1981-82 to 1998-99.
2. Annual Reports of all Sugar Factories in Marathwada.

per year. The cane crushed in the district is found to have increased at the annual rate of 26.33 per cent. For Jalna district the quantity of cane crushed was 0.91 lakh metric tonnes in 1984-85, which went up to 3.94 lakh metric tonnes in 1998-99. It increased at the annual average growth rate of 24.62 per cent during the study period. The annual average growth rate of cane crushed in case of Parbhani district was 17.94 per cent with an average crushed quantity of 5.01 lakh metric tonnes per year during the study period. For Beed district the per year cane crushed was 6.97 lakh metric tonnes. It is found to have increased at the simple annual growth rate of 6.15 per cent during the study period.

Table 2
Districtwise Sugarcane Crushed in Marathwada During 1981-82 to 1998-99

(lakh metric tonnes)

Year	*Aurangabad*	*Jalna*	*Parbhani*	*Beed*	*Nanded*	*Osmanabad*	*Latur*
1981-82	13.67	-	3.98	8.85	4.28	5.25	2.47
1982-83	11.68	-	5.06	8.31	4.71	4.44	1.98
1983-84	0.62	-	1.25	3.62	1.38	1.53	0.93
1984-85	9.78	0.91	4.07	5.88	2.45	3.91	1.93
1985-86	6.12	1.29	3.71	5.75	2.00	2.86	2.41
1986-87	4.56	1.07	2.84	5.21	1.76	2.28	1.90
1987-88	7.21	1.99	4.96	5.35	3.16	2.39	4.06
1988-89	7.78	3.01	4.21	7.43	3.39	5.42	4.89
1989-90	15.76	5.50	7.63	12.09	7.04	8.11	8.31
1990-91	16.23	6.63	7.96	11.72	8.56	8.26	7.83
1991-92	14.16	6.04	8.07	9.42	6.92	6.84	8.33
1992-93	9.08	4.14	5.06	1.92	3.06	3.80	4.74
1993-94	7.09	3.29	4.38	0.92	4.34	2.19	6.14
1994-95	15.38	6.67	9.13	10.56	8.84	8.87	11.32
1995-96	15.57	6.92	7.40	9.01	7.38	8.81	9.23
1996-97	6.21	1.94	3.32	2.71	4.19	5.31	7.43
1997-98	2.16.	1.89	2.94	7.49	2.30	7.59	9.87
1998-99	10.57	3.94	4.15	9.17	5.21	8.10	9.28
Average	9.98	3.68	5.01	6.97	4.50	5.33	5.74
Simple annual growth rate (%)	26.33	24.62	17.94	6.15	17.34	24.75	17.91

Sources: 1. Working Results of Sugar Factories in Maharashtra, Vasantdada Sugar Institute, Pune, 1981-82 to 1998-99.
2. Annual Reports of all Sugar Factories in Marathwada.

The sugar factories in Nanded district had crushed 4.28 lakh metric tonnes of cane in 1981-82 which increased up to 5.21 lakh metric tonnes in 1998-99, with an average annual growth rate of 17.34 per cent during the study period. This district has crushed on an average 4.50 lakh metric tonnes cane per year. In case of Osmanabad district the quantity of cane crushed was 5.25 lakh metric tonnes in 1981-82, which increased up to 8.10 lakh metric tonnes in 1998-99, with an average annual growth rate of 24.75 per cent. This district has crushed 5.33 lakh metric tonnes of sugarcane per year during the study period. In Latur district the quantity of cane crushed by sugar factories was 2.47 lakh metric tonnes in 1981-82 and 9.28 lakh metric tonnes in 1998-99. The sugar factories in this district had crushed 5.74 lakh metric tonnes cane per year. The sugarcane crushed in this district has grown at the annual rate of 17.91 per cent during the study period.

If we consider the whole period, it is seen that the per year sugarcane crushed is found to be the highest in case of Aurangabad district (i.e. 9.98 metric tonnes) followed by Beed district (i.e. 6.97 lakh metric tonnes), Jalna district lies at the bottom in case of sugarcane crushed per year during the same period. The quantity of cane crushed per year in Parbhani, Nanded, Osmanabad and Latur districts was near about 5 lakh metric tonnes during the study period. The average annual growth rate of cane crushed was the highest in case of Aurangabad district i.e. 26.33 per cent due to more production of sugarcane and crushing capacity of factories and it was the lowest in case of Beed district i.e. 6.15 per cent, per year during the period under consideration.

GROWTH TRENDS IN SUGAR OUTPUT

Table 3 shows the data about the sugar output in Marathwada during 1981-82 to 1998-99. During 1981-82 sugar output in Marathwada was 36.74 lakh quintals, which increased and reached up to 56.01 lakh quintals in 1998-99. The sugar output in Marathwada was the highest of 71.62 lakh quintals in 1994-95 and the lowest of 16.07 lakh quintals in 1983-84. The mean sugar production in Marathwada is found to be 41.74 lakh quintals during the study period. The sugar output in Marathwada is found to have grown at the annual rate of 16.25 per cent during the period under study.

Table 4 shows the districtwise data about sugar output produced by sugar factories in Marathwada region during 1981-82 to 1998-99. The mean sugar output produced in Aurangabad district was 10.34 lakh quintals for the whole period. The growth rate of sugar output for this district is

Table 3
Sugar Output Produced by Sugar Factories in Marathwada During 1980-81 to 1998-99

(In lakh quintals)

Year	*Sugar output*
1981-82	36.74
1982-83	37.70
1983-84	16.07
1984-85	30.32
1985-86	25.08
1986-87	19.07
1987-88	28.67
1988-89	36.57
1989-90	65.99
1990-91	71.05
1991-92	64.11
1992-93	33.81
1993-94	29.18
1994-95	71.62
1995-96	62.60
1996-97	34.24
1997-98	32.55
1998-99	56.01
Average	41.74
Simple annual growth rate (%)	16.25

Sources: 1. Working Results of Sugar Factories in Maharashtra, Vasantdada Sugar Institute, Pune, 1981-82 to 1998-99.
2. Annual Reports of all Sugar Factories in Marathwada.

found to be very high i.e. 58.92 per cent. The sugar factories in Jalna district have produced 4.16 lakh quintals of sugar per year during the study period. Sugar factories in Parbhani district have produced 5.30 lakh quintals of sugar per year, with an average annual growth rate of 20.55 per cent during the study period. The average annual growth rate of sugar output produced in Beed district was 42.69 per cent. The sugar factories of this district have produced 6.21 lakh quintals of sugar per year during the study period. The lowest sugar output produced in this district was only 0.78 lakh quintals in 1993-94 and highest output of 11.81 lakh quintals was found in 1989-90.

Table 4
Districtwise Sugar Output Produced by the Sugar Factories in Marathwada During 1981-82 to 1998-99

(In lakh quintals)

Year	*Aurangabad*	*Jalna*	*Parbhani*	*Beed*	*Nanded*	*Osmanabad*	*Latur*
1981-82	13.21	-	3.89	8.25	3.89	5.38	2.12
1982-83	12.31	-	6.59	7.59	4.54	4.50	2.18
1983-84	7.09	-	1.30	3.76	1.39	1.58	0.95
1984-85	10.53	0.93	4.35	6.07	2.40	4.07	1.96
1985-86	6.36	1.31	4.02	5.94	1.88	3.11	2.45
1986-87	4.51	1.05	2.82	5.20	1.63	2.20	1.65
1987-88	7.11	1.90	5.09	5.39	3.00	2.31	3.88
1988-89	7.83	3.07	4.58	7.64	3.51	4.88	5.06
1989-90	15.97	5.44	8.52	11.81	7.35	8.00	8.90
1990-91	17.31	6.76	8.47	11.59	8.92	8.25	9.77
1991-92	15.28	6.38	8.76	9.38	7.70	7.17	9.43
1992-93	9.72	4.45	5.51	2.11	3.15	3.76	5.13
1993-94	7.31	3.32	4.59	0.87	4.36	1.97	6.76
1994-95	15.68	6.57	9.18	1.05	8.24	9.08	12.41
1995-96	15.52	7.03	7.04	8.08	6.61	7.76	10.55
1996-97	8.01	2.29	3.34	2.81	4.41	5.31	8.07
1997-98	1.04	1.95	3.02	4.76	2.18	8.17	11.43
1998-99	11.29	5.80	4.32	9.53	5.14	9.08	10.84
Average	10.34	4.16	5.30	6.21	4.46	5.37	6.31
Simple annual growth rate (%)	58.92	32.60	20.55	42.69	16.86	28.14	21.21

Sources: 1. Working Results of Sugar Factories in Maharashtra, Vasantdada Sugar Institute, Pune, 1981-82 to 1998-99.
2. Annual Reports of all sugar factories in Marathwada.

In case of Nanded district, the production of sugar was 3.89 lakh quintals in 1981-82, which increased up to 5.14 lakh quintals in 1998-99. On an average, the sugar factories in Nanded district have produced 4.46 lakh quintals of sugar per year during the period under study. The simple annual growth rate of sugar output in the district was 16.86 per cent. The simple annual growth rate of sugar output in case of Osmanabad district was 28.14 per cent. Sugar factories in Osmanabad district have produced, on an average, 5.37

lakh quintals of sugar per year during the study period. In case of Latur district, the sugar factories have produced 6.31 lakh quintals of sugar per year during the study period. Growth rate of sugar output in Latur district is found to be 21.21 per cent per annum.

Among the seven districts the sugar factories of Aurangabad district have produced the highest sugar output followed by sugar factories in Latur and Beed districts. Jalna district lies at the bottom with respect to sugar production. Aurangabad district indicates highest growth in sugar output followed by Beed and Jalna districts in that order during the study period.

TRENDS IN SUGAR RECOVERY

The ratio of the total quantity of sugar produced and the total quantity of sugarcane crushed expressed in terms of percentage is termed as recovery percentage of sugar, in a sugar factory. Since this is the ratio which is related to the output of sugar in a sugar factory from the sugarcane crushed, it could be taken as an indicator of efficiency in a sugar factory. The recovery of sugar depends on large number of factors. The content of sugar in sugarcane crop is the result of agro-climatic factors and also other agronomic and cultural practices adopted in cultivation of sugarcane. The time of planting, variety planted, irrigation, manuring and fertilization of the crop, insect and disease control measures taken and the climatic and soil conditions are some of these factors relating to the cultivation of sugarcane crop, which has the bearing on the sugar content. The other group of factors include the harvesting of the sugarcane at maturity stage and its transportation to the sugar factory without allowing the dry-age of the sugarcane before it is fed to the factory for crushing. The harvesting of sugarcane without leaving any stalk underground also proved to increase the sugar recovery.

Table 5 shows the data about recovery percentage of sugar in Marathwada region during 1981-82 to 1998-99.

Table 5
Recovery Percentage of Sugar in Marathwada During 1981-82 to 1998-99

Year	*Percentage of Recovery*
1981-82	9.37
1982-83	10.18
1983-84	10.25
1984-85	10.28
1985-86	10.22
1986-87	9.08
1987-88	9.69
1988-89	10.30
1989-90	10.12
1990-91	10.44
1991-92	10.69
1992-93	10.50
1993-94	9.94
1994-95	9.97
1995-96	9.59
1996-97	10.12
1997-98	9.92
1998-99	10.47
Average	10.06
Simple annual growth rate (%)	0.78

Sources: 1. Working Results of Sugar Factories in Maharashtra, Vasantdada Sugar Institute, Pune, 1981-82 to 1998-99.
2. Annual Reports of all Sugar Factories in Marathwada.

In 1981-82 the percentage of sugar recovery in Marathwada was 9.37 per cent which increased and reached upto 10.47 per cent in 1998-99. During the decade 1981-82 to 1990-91 the percentage recovery of sugar in Marathwada varied between a very low range of 9.08 per cent in 1986-87 to 10.44 per cent in 1990-91. On an average, the percentage of recovery in Marathwada was 10.06 per cent during the whole period under study, and the sugar recovery in Marathwada has improved over the period at the annual average rate of 0.78 per cent.

Table 6 gives information about districtwise recovery percentage of sugar in Marathwada region during 1981-82

Table 6
Districtwise Recovery Percentage of Sugar in Marathwada During 1981-82 to 1998-99

Year	*Auranga-bad*	*Jalna*	*Parbhani*	*Beed*	*Nanded*	*Osmanabad*	*Latur*
1981-82	9.67	–	9.61	9.64	8.92	9.73	8.62
1982-83	10.51	–	10.41	9.85	9.55	10.01	10.77
1983-84	10.60	–	10.40	10.33	9.65	10.32	10.22
1984-85	10.66	10.38	10.64	10.31	9.61	10.28	10.12
1985-86	10.41	10.18	10.70	10.21	9.36	10.89	9.77
1986-87	9.89	8.75	9.70	9.89	9.27	7.24	8.84
1987-88	9.89	9.56	10.18	9.91	9.26	9.57	9.47
1988-89	9.96	10.21	10.82	10.22	10.08	10.48	10.37
1989-90	10.04	9.89	10.41	9.68	10.26	9.87	10.72
1990-91	10.71	10.19	10.61	9.85	10.66	9.97	11.07
1991-92	10.82	10.58	10.79	10.23	10.62	10.50	11.26
1992-93	10.70	10.75	10.69	10.85	10.26	8,76	19.37
1993-94	10.30	10.08	9.63	9.45	9.87	9.53	10.75
1994-95	10.,16	9.85	9.93	9.93	9.24	10.07	10.62
1995-96	9.95	9.93	9.35	8.95	8.75	9.62	10.58
1996-97	9.83	10.60	9.41	9.32	10.03	10.21	11.41
1997-98	9.66	10.22	9.66	9.91	9.09	10.57	10.37
1998-99	9.66	10.56	10.38	10.48	9.70	10.68	11.87
Average	10.19	8.43	10.18	9.95	9.68	9.97	10.4
Simple annual growth rate (%)	-0.03	0.46	0.35	2.70	0.66	1.68	2.25

Sources: 1. Working Results of Sugar Factories in Maharashtra, Vasantdada Sugar Institute, Pune, 1981-82 to 1998-99.
2. Annual Reports of all Sugar Factories in Marathwada.

to 1998-99. From this table it can be seen that, Aurangabad and Parbhani districts show a very high recovery percentage (i.e. 10.19 and 10.18 per cent respectively) followed by Latur, Osmanabad, Beed, Nanded and at last Jalna district. Aurangabad, Parbhani and Latur districts have achieved a recovery level higher than 10 per cent during the study period and remaining four districts have enjoyed recovery percentage of sugar as Jalna 8.43 per cent, Beed 9.85 per cent, Nanded 9.68 per cent and Osmanabad 9.97 per cent during the period under study. The table 6 also indicates that the recovery percentage of sugar varied between 8.43

per cent in Jalna and 10.44 per cent in Aurangabad district during the study period. In case of all the districts in Marathwada, the growth rate of sugar recovery has been positive except Aurangabad district. In case of Beed and Latur districts the annual growth rate of sugar recovery is found to be higher (i.e. 2.70 per cent and 2.25 per cent respectively) followed by Osmanabad district (1.68 per cent), Nanded (0.66 per cent), Jalna (0.46 per cent), Parbhani (0.35 per cent) and Aurangabad district has experienced a negative but insignificant growth [(-) 0.03 per cent] in sugar recovery during the study period. Among the seven districts, the sugar recovery for Aurangabad district was the highest due to better transportation facilities and better quality of sugarcane in this district. In case of Jalna district the recovery percentage is found to be lower than other districts because of low quality of sugarcane, less transportation facilities and high time loss between cutting and crushing of sugarcane. For the whole period, the growth in percentage of sugar recovery is found to be the highest in case of Beed district (i.e. 2.70 per cent per annum) and the lowest in case of Aurangabad district (-0.03 per cent per annum). From the above it can be concluded that there has been tremendous improvement in the sugar recovery in Beed district.

To sum up, sugarcane is one of the important cash crops grown in India. Maharashtra is one of the major sugarcane producing states in India. Importance of sugarcane as a commercial crop has grown considerably during the last two decades in the country and particularly in the Maharashtra State.

In this study, it is found that the average sugarcane crushed per year is the highest in case of Aurangabad district (i.e. 9.98 metric tonnes). Jalna district lies at the bottom in case of average sugarcane crushed per year during the study period. The sugar output has grown at the annual rate of 16.25 per cent in Marathwada during the period under study. Among the seven districts the sugar factories of Aurangabad district have produced the highest sugar output followed by sugar factories in Latur district, and Beed district lies at the bottom in this respect. Also the sugar factories in Aurangabad district have indicated the highest growth in sugar output followed by sugar factories in Beed and Jalna districts in that order during the study period.

References

1. Thakare R.P., Veerkar P.D. and Joshi R.M., Regional Trends in Area, Production and Productivity of Sugarcane and Acreage Response in Maharashtra State, Maharashtra Journal of Agricultural Economics, Vol. VII, No. 1, March, 1995.
2. Agnihotri C.B., Sugarcane Cultivation in India, Bharatiya Sugar Directory, 1987.

6

Impact of Sugar Cooperatives on Economic Development

The cooperative sugar factories, as the farmers' organization have emerged as a leading force to give directions to the development of the rural areas. These factories did not remain only as the cooperative agroprocessing units, but have become the centres of rural development. The cooperative sugar factories have provided employment to the large number of workers in the village countryside. In the process of working of the sugar factories the effects on the growth of other ancillary industries and ancillary activities are also seen. The small and medium size industries producing the machinery parts, chemicals have developed in area, likewise the industries based on the waste products of the sugar factories have been developed in some areas. Thus the backward and forward linkages in the process of economic development have been and are being established, because of the cooperative sugar factories.

The cooperative sugar factories have also tried to meet the social obligation by taking many development schemes in the operational areas. They have been playing important role in the implementation of 20-point programme of economic development. These factories have opened schools, colleges, educational institutions including technical education. In Maharashtra two cooperative sugar factories have started medical colleges and quite a few of the cooperative sugar factories, have started the engineering colleges. The role of cooperative sugar factories in irrigation and thereby in agricultural development is noteworthy. The sugar factories realized the importance of saving of the forest and as a part of the programme large number of biogas plants have been supplied by the sugar factories to the farmers in their area of operation, with the aid of the financing institutions and the state government. Many cooperative sugar factories have undertaken the programme of afforestation and development of forests in their areas.

The Council for Social Development undertook the in-depth study in March 1981, by a team of experts, headed by Dr. B. Venkatappaiah. They studied the socio-economic impact of the cooperative sugar factories. The observations made by the council, regarding the impact of the cooperative sugar factories in Maharashtra are of a great significance. It has been brought out that the cooperative sugar factories have played significant role in the sugarcane development, increasing the saving habits of the members and providing additional sources of income to vulnerable section of the community in their area of operation. They have further observed that the cooperative sugar factories in Maharashtra have played a major role in poultry development, lift irrigation development and implementation of various points under 20-point programme of economic development[1].

The National Cooperative Development Corporation conducted the study of the impact of cooperative sugar factories in rural development and the findings of the study were also almost same as that of Venkatappaiah Committee. The National Cooperative Development Corporation compiled the report on the impact of cooperative sugar factories on rural development, which has concluded that the cooperative sugar factories in Maharashtra have played the role of rural development and these factories have emerged as centres of rural development[2].

The role of cooperative sugar factories in rural development is the outcome of its involvement into the problems of the rural areas and the awareness of the problems of the rural area by the management of the cooperative sugar factories. This role has been played effectively and with spectacular results by the cooperative sugar factories, which are successfully working as an agro-processing units. The adequate sugarcane availability, position of exploiting full crushing capacity, satisfactory recovery percentage etc. are some of the factors which make it possible to a cooperative sugar factory to play active role in the rural development. Since there is a large variation from one factory to the other in respect of working results, there is bound to be the variation between the work done by one factory in the field of socio-economic development from that of the other. The sugar factories which could not achieve satisfactory working results and are incurring losses year after year cannot undertake any activity of rural development.

The cooperative sugar factories from Marathwada, selected for the present study, are facing the shortage of sugarcane supply and incurring heavy losses, year after year, except one. In the light of the working results of these factories, the area development work done by these factories was also not comparable with that of the factories from western Maharashtra. These factories are however, trying to do some work in the field of rural development. The work done by these factories in the field of rural development, will surely improve with the improvement in the working results. The work done by cooperative sugar factories can be grouped into two major categories viz. work of agricultural development and the work of other socio-economic development. The central government also regulates the wages and conditions of service of the clerical manual and supervisory personnel in the cooperative sugar factories and levies excise and income tax on them[3]. In this chapter an attempt is made to examine the employment requirement, agricultural development, welfare measures and social security scheme by the sugar factories in Marathwada.

EMPLOYMENT IN SUGAR INDUSTRY IN MARATHWADA

Employment Requirement

A sugar factory requires permanent and seasonal staff. The staff of the factory can be further classified into administrative, technical, skilled, semi-skilled and unskilled categories. The availability of this personnel (especially seasonally employed skilled personnel) at the right time is a very important factor governing the economic working of a factory.

The various categories of workers found in cooperative sugar factories are as under:

1. Permanent–workers who get full time job for the whole year without any break,
2. Seasonal–workers are employed only in crushing season. The workers get retention allowance during the off season. Immigrant seasonal harvesting labour is not included in it.
3. Temporary–Workers who get work for some days in a year especially in crushing season and sometimes in off season. These workers do not get retention allowance during the off season.

The staff in the agricultural department in these factories, right from the Chief Agricultural Officer to that of the slip boys are engaged in the area of operation of the sugar factories for contracting non-member sugarcane. During off season, they are also engaged in other tasks of contracting the harvesting and transporting labour and making arrangements before the start of crushing season for the supply of sugarcane to their factories. The same staff is also looking after the nursery farm of the factory and some stray programmes of seed distribution, seed treatment etc.

undertaken by the factories as sporadic programmes. There is no pattern of staffing followed in these factories in sugarcane development department. Some officers from the agriculture department itself are designated like Cane Development officer, Assistant Cane Development Officer and the like without adequate supporting staff.

The Directorate of Sugar, Maharashtra State, Pune, has issued detailed circular to all cooperative sugar factories in Maharashtra in 1984, suggesting therein measures for sugarcane development and the pattern of staff which cooperative sugar factories should have in their sugarcane development departments. It is suggested, in this circular that the sugarcane development department should be headed by an expert in the field of sugarcane development and may be designated as Agricultural Development Officer. He should be assisted by one agronomist, one crop protection officer, one soil scientist and one technical officer. There should be agricultural development assistants qualified in the field of agriculture and their number should be one office for each 200 hectares of the area under sugarcane or proposed to be developed under cane. In addition there should be agricultural assistant one for each 50 to 100 hectares area under sugarcane. This wing will be incharge of the nursery farm, soil testing laboratory, seed multiplication programme, plant protection including seed treatment, extension work relating to sugarcane technology and all other work relating to cane development[4].

Permanent and Seasonal Employment

If a sugar factory is established in some region it provides employment opportunities for five to six thousand workers approximately. The factory requires seven to eight hundred skilled and unskilled workers for the production of sugar. They are temporary, permanent and seasonal. In addition to this, for harvesting and transporting sugarcane from field to factory near about five thousand workers are required. Of course, the proportion of workers depends upon the crushing capacity of the sugar factory.

Table 1 shows the number of workers employed in the sugar factories in Marathwada in 1988-89 and 1998-99. The factorywise employment data shown in this table reveals that out of 22 sugar factories selected for the present study, a sugar factory with 1250 tonnes daily crushing capacity has provided employment to 365 persons and seasonal employment to 343 persons, a sugar factory with 2500 tonnes daily crushing capacity has provided permanent employment to 461 persons and seasonal employment to 417 persons, and a sugar factory with 3500 tonnes daily crushing capacity has provided permanent employment to 646 persons and seasonal employment to 653 persons. In 1987-88, the sugar factories in Aurangabad district had provided employment to quite huge number of workers i.e. 3387 and next to this sugar factories in Beed district provided employment to 2645 workers and the lowest employment of 1140 was provided by Jalna district sugar factories. In case of both permanent and seasonal employment, the sugar factories in Aurangabad district ranked first while sugar factories in Beed district were at the bottom in the year 1987-88. In 1998-99, the sugar factories in Aurangabad district have provided employment to quite huge number of workers (i.e. 3844) and next to this by sugar factories in Parbhani district have provided employment to 2588 workers. The sugar factories in Jalna district have provided the lowest employment i.e. 1248 in the year 1998-99. The employment of permanent workers is found to be the highest in case of sugar factories in Aurangabad district (2267) and the lowest in case of sugar factories in Jalna district (802). The seasonal employment is found to be the highest in case of Osmanabad district (1666) and the lowest in case of Jalna district (446) in 1998-99.

Additional Employment Generated by the Sugar Factories in the Marathwada Region for Harvesting Labours

In this section the extent of excess production of sugarcane and the excess capacity utilization during 1990-91 and 1995-96 have been initially discussed. During 1990-91 the average

Table 1
Districtwise Employment by Sugar Factories in Marathwada in 1987-88 and 1998-99

Sr. No.	District	No. of permanent employees		Increase/ decrease	No. of seasonal employees		Increase/ decrease	Total employment		Increase/ decrease
		1987-88	1998-99		1987-88	1998-99		1987-88	1998-99	
1.	Aurangabad	1819	2267	448	1618	1577	-41	3387	3844	457
2.	Jalna	648	802	154	492	446	-46	1140	1248	108
3.	Beed	1524	1506	-18	1121	975	-146	2645	2481	-164
4.	Parbhani	979	1289	310	892	1299	407	1871	2588	717
5.	Nanded	1070	1058	-12	1035	1029	-6	2105	2087	-18
6.	Osmanabad	1102	1051	-51	1040	1666	626	2120	1707	-413
7.	Latur	1289	1190	-99	1330	970	-360	2619	2160	-459
8.	Marathwada	8431	9163	732	7528	7962	434	15887	16115	228

Source: Maharashtra Rajya Sahakari Sakhar Karkhana Sangh Ltd., Mumbai, Information for 4th and 5th December 1999 meeting.

crushing days were 236. It means that according to the state norms the sugar factories had additional 76 days. During 1995-96 the average working days were 213. It means that according to the state norms (160 days) there were 53 additional crushing days in this year. On the basis of this the additional employment generated by sugar factories during the excess sugarcane crop years have been calculated.

Generally, half of the sugarcane quantity required was supplied (transported and harvested) by bullock carts and the remaining half by tractors and trucks. A bullock cart on an average can carry 1.25 metric tonnes of sugarcane which requires five to six labourers approximately. A tractor has the capacity of transporting cane to the tune of 6 metric tonnes at the maximum which requires a minimum 12 labourers, and a truck on an average transports 12 metric tonnes of sugarcane which requires a minimum 25 labourers. By taking into account the quantity transported by these means and the labourers required to harvest and for loading and unloading of sugarcane, a sugar factory having a crushing capacity of 1,250 tonnes per day, requires a minimum of 4,250 harvesting labourers. For a single factory with crushing capacity of 2,000 tonnes requires 6,800 harvesting labourers, a factory with crushing capacity of 2,500 tonnes requires 8,500 harvesting labourers, and for a factory with crushing capacity of 3,500 tonnes requires 11,900 harvesting labourers.

Table 2 gives an idea of the excess employment generated as per the state norms. It has already been explained that for 100 per cent capacity utilization of a sugar factory, a sugar factory must work for 160 days in a year as per state norms. While calculating the additional employment generated by the sugar factory, the excess working days are calculated by deducting the required number of days, as per the state norms, from the actual working days of the season. Thereafter, for calculating the additional employment, the total excess working days are multiplied by the number of harvesting labours employed. Thus, the additional employment generated in terms of mandays during 1990-91 was 89,10,550 days as per the state norms.

Table 2
Districtwise Additional Employment Generated for Harvesting Labourers During 1990-91 and 1995-96 Crushing Seasons in Marathwada

Sr. No.	*District*	*Per day minimum required harvest labours*	*Working days of sugar factory*	*Excess crushing days as per state norms (160 days)*	*Additional employment generated (Days)*
		1990-91			
1.	Aurangabad	26350	1131	331	1748450
2.	Jalna	8500	468	148	629000
3.	Beed	21250	1007	367	1921000
4.	Parbhani	17000	710	230	1309000
5.	Nanded	12750	711	231	981750
6.	Osmanabad	16150	473	153	1407600
7.	Latur	12750	695	215	913750
8.	Marathwada	114750	5195	1675	8910550
	Average	5216	236	76	405025
		1995-96			
1.	Aurangabad	30600	1047	247	1483250
2.	Jalna	12750	447	127	884000
3.	Beed	2550	836	196	1211250
4.	Parbhani	17000	621	141	828750
5.	Nanded	17000	659	179	1037000
6.	Osmanabad	16150	436	117	1078650
7.	Latur	12750	636	156	663000
8.	Marathwada	114750	4683	1163	7185900
	Average	5216	213	53	326631

Sources: 1. Annual Reports of All Sugar Factories in Marathwada.
2. The Report of the Committee for Recommending a Package for Rehabilitation of Sick Factories in Cooperative Sector, Published by Government of Maharashtra, June 1990, Appendix XII- 7.

In the same way the excess working days and additional employment generated by the sugar factories during 1995-96 was calculated. The average working days were 213 and the excess working days were 53, as per state norms. The additional employment generated as per the state level norms was 71,85,900 days. The per factory additional employment generated is 4,05,025 days in 1990-91 and 3,26,631 days in 1995-96.

The data about employment generated for harvesting labour in 1990-91 and 1998-99 are shown in table 3.

Table 3
District-wise Employment Generated for Harvesting Labourers During 1990-91 and 1998-99 Seasons in Marathwada

Sr. No.	*District*	*1990-91 Per day minimum required harvest labourers*	*1998-99 Per day minimum required harvest labourers*
1.	Aurangabad	26350	30600
2.	Jalna	8500	12750
3.	Beed	21250	25500
4.	Parbhani	17000	12750
5.	Nanded	12750	17000
6.	Osmanabad	16150	16150
7.	Latur	12750	12750
8.	Marathwada	114750	127500
	Average	5216	6071

Sources: 1. Annual Reports of All Sugar Factories in Marathwada.
2. The Report of the Committee for Recommending a Package for Rehabilitation of Sick Sugar Factories in Cooperative Sector, Published by Government of Maharashtra, June 1990, Appendix XII-7.

When crushing season is extended for a longer period, the sugar factories can provide employment to harvesting labours for more days. During 1990-91 and 1998-99, all the sugar factories in Marathwada region provided more days of employment to their harvesting labours. The average harvesting labours of the sugar factories in Marathwada region is estimated to be 5,216 per day in 1990-91. The average harvesting labours of the sugar factories in Marathwada region is estimated to be 6,071 per day in 1998-99. As per the state norms all the districts in Marathwada region generated employment of 1,14,750 in 1990-91 and 1,27,500 of harvesting labours in 1998-99. Thus, it can be said that the generation of employment to harvesting and seasonal workers is the positive impact of excess sugarcane crop.

Additional Employment Generated for Seasonal Workers by Sugar Factories in the Marathwada Region

Almost all the sugar factories employ seasonal workers during crushing season. But, when crushing season is extended for a longer period, the sugar factories can provide employment to seasonal workers for more days.

Table 4 indicates that all the sugar factories in Marathwada region provided more days of employment to their seasonal workers during 1990-91 and 1995-96. The average seasonal employment of the districts in Marathwada region is 340. As per the state norms the sugar factories in Marathwada region generated additional employment of 5,91,260 days and 3,95,420 days during 1990-91 and 1995-96 respectively. Thus, it can be said that generation of additional employment to harvesting and seasonal workers is the positive impact of excess sugarcane crop.

Table 4
District-wise Additional Employment Generated for Seasonal Labourers During 1990-91 and 1995-96 Seasons in Marathwada

Sr. No.	*District*	*Crushing days*	*1990-91 Excess crushing days as per state norms (160 days)*	*Average seasonal employment (Days)*	*Additional employment as per state norms (Days)*
1.	Aurangabad	1131	331	1700	112540
2.	Jalna	468	148	680	40320
3.	Beed	1027	367	1360	124780
4.	Parbhani	710	230	1020	78200
5.	Nanded	711	231	1020	78540
6.	Osmanabad	473	153	680	52020
7.	Latur	695	215	1020	73100
8.	Marathwada	5195	1675	7480	591260
	Average	236	76	340	26876

Contd...

Table 4 Contd.

Sr. No.	*District*	*Crushing days*	*1990-91 Excess crushing days as per state norms (160 days)*	*Average seasonal employ-ment (Days)*	*Additional employment as per state norms (Days)*
			1995-96		
1.	Aurangabad	1047	247	1700	783980
2.	Jalna	447	127	680	43180
3.	Beed	836	196	1360	66640
4.	Parbhani	621	141	1020	47940
5.	Nanded	659	179	1020	60860
6.	Osmanabad	437	117	680	39780
7.	Latur	636	156	1020	53040
8.	Marathwada	4683	1163	7480	395420
	Average	213	53	340	17974

Sources: 1. Annual Reports of All Sugar Factories in Marathwada.
2. The Report of the Committee for Recommending a Package for Rehabilitation of Sick Sugar Factories in Cooperative Sector, Published by Government of Maharashtra, June 1990, Appendix XXI-7.

AGRICULTURAL DEVELOPMENT

The cooperative sugar factories depend on the raw material produced by their members. Therefore, as a part of their effort to obtain adequate raw material, these factories have taken steps in increasing irrigation potential and also the steps for agricultural development of their areas.

Irrigation Development

The large number of minor, medium and major irrigation projects have been completed in Marathwada. The advantages of backwater are available to the areas on the upstream of the irrigation projects. There is a provision for lifting water from such backwater of the various irrigation projects. Likewise, the permission to lift water from the canals for lift irrigation of the area which is not irrigable by the command of the canal, can be obtained from the concerned authorities within the permissible limits. The sugar factories which have the advantages of the backwater of some irrigation projects or the canal, in their area, are taking steps to organise the lift irrigation schemes for increasing the area under irrigation. Generally the cooperative sugar factories perform the promotional role in organisation of the lift irrigation scheme and completing the same. The permission of water lifting is pursued by the cooperative sugar factories. The farmers in the area are made aware of the advantages of the lift irrigation schemes and they are organised either into groups or cooperative lift irrigation societies. The loan applications are also made by the sugar factories and the sanction of loan is pursued with the concerned banks. In some cases the lift irrigation schemes are totally owned by the cooperative sugar factories.

Irrigation water is important input in sugarcane production. Sugarcane cropping area depends upon availability of irrigation water. The information about irrigation sources, area irrigated by different sources like wells, lift irrigation schemes, bandharas/K.T. weirs/ percolation tanks etc. and area under micro-irrigation techniques in sugarcane from the operational area of each sugar factory in Marathwada was collected from them. The districtwise compiled picture of irrigation with different sources is presented in table 5.

In Aurangabad district, based on the information of three sugar factories, the total operational area was 4,32,094 hectares and irrigated area was 1,07,722 hectares i.e. 24.93 per cent. The area irrigated by wells, canals, lift irrigation and K.T. weirs/bandharas was 86,635 hectares, 17951 hectares, 2353 hectares and 783 hectares respectively. The percentage to irrigated area by these sources comes to 80.42 per cent, 16.66 per cent, 2.18 per cent and 0.74 per cent respectively. The area under drip was hardly 5 hectares.

In Jalna district, based on information from two factories, out of total irrigated area of 78,188.65 hectares, area under wells, canals, lift irrigation and bandharas was 36,864.65 hectares, 32,800 hectares, 1,207 hectares and 7,317 hectares respectively. The area under surface drip irrigation system in sugarcane was 104 hectares.

As per the information in full received only from Purna S.S.K. Ltd. in Parbhani district, out of total operational area of 1,20,762 hectares the irrigated area was 45,673 hectares. The area irrigated by wells, canals and lift irrigation was 4267 hectares, 40718 hectares and 688 hectares respectively which comes to 9.34 per cent, 89.15 per cent and 1.07 per cent respectively compared to the total irrigated area.

In Beed district, the complete information was received only from two sugar factories. Out of total operational area of 5,09,376.4 hectares, the irrigated area was only 30,595.9 hectares. The area under wells was 82.07 per cent i.e. 25,111 hectares, under canals was 2,828 hectares i.e. 9.24 per cent, under lift irrigation schemes was 960 hectares i.e. 3.14 per cent and area under bandharas/K.T. weirs was about 5.55 per cent i.e. 1,696.9 hectares. The area under surface drip irrigation system was reported to be 75.40 hectares.

Table 5
Information About Irrigation Sources and Area Under Micro-Irrigation in the Sugar Factories Area in Marathwada (1995-96).

Sr. No.	*District*	*Total operational area (hectares)*	*Total area irrigated by wells (open+bore) (hectares)*	*Area irrigated by canals (hectares)*	*Area irrigated by lift irrigation scheme (hectares)*
1.	Aurangabad	4,32,094	86,635 (80.42)	17,951 (16.66)	2,353 (2.18)
2.	Jalna	N.A.	36,864.65 (47.15)	32,800 (41.95)	1,207 (1.54)
3.	Parbhani	1,20,762	4,267 (9.34)	40,718 (89.15)	688 (1.07)
4.	Beed	5,09,376.4	25,111 (82.07)	2,828 (9.24)	960 (3.14)
5.	Latur	N.A.	37,200 (67.02)	4,000 (7.20)	10,000 (18.02)
6.	Nanded	7,12,000	13,771 (10.89)	–	1,12,589 (89.01)
7.	Osmanabad	5,29,310	45,597 (59.24)	–	31,361 (40.76)
	Marathwada	2303542.40	249445	98297	159158

Table 5 Contd.

Sr. No.	*District*	*Area irrigated by bhandaras / K.T. weirs / Percolation tanks (hectares)*	*Total irrigated area in the district (hectares)*	*Area Under Micro-Irrigation (hectares)*		
				Surface drip	*Sub-surface drip*	*Total area under drip*
1.	Aurangabad	783 (0.74)	1,07,722	5	–	5
2.	Jalna	7,317 (9.36)	78,188.65	104	–	104
3.	Parbhani	N.A.	45,673	–	–	–
4.	Beed	1,696.90 (5.55)	30,595.9	7540	–	75.40
5.	Latur	4300 (7.75)	55,500	40	40	80
6.	Nanded	N.A.	1,26,360	–	–	–
7.	Osmanabad	N.A.	76,958	–	–	–
	Marathwada	1409690	450627.55	7689	40	264.40

Figures in parenthesis indicate percentage to total irrigated area.
Source: The Role of Biotechnology in Sugarcane Productivity and Sustainability, XII Annual State Level Sugarcane Development Workshop, Vasantdada Sugar Institute, Pune, 18-19 August, 1995.

In Nanded district, based on information from three sugar factories out of total irrigated area of 1,26,360 hectares, area under wells and lift irrigation was 13,771 and 1,12,589 hectares respectively. In Osmanabad district, based on information from two sugar factories out of total irrigated area of 76,958 hectares, area under wells and lift irrigation was 45,597 hectares and 31,361 hectares respectively. In Latur district, based on information from two sugar factories out of total irrigated area of 55,500 hectares, area under wells, canals, lift irrigation and bandharas was 37,200 hectares, 4,000 hectares, 10,000 hectares and 4,300 hectares respectively. The area under surface and sub-surface drip irrigation system was 40 hectares each.

Improved Varieties of Seeds

Sugarcane is vegetatively propagated crop and therefore the seed quality is most important factor, affecting the yield of

Table 6
Districtwise Information About Requirement of Seed Area in Marathwada (1995-96)

Sr. No.	Particulars	Auran-gabad	Jalna	Beed	Parbhani	Nanded	Osmana-bad	Latur	Marath-wada
1.	Total number of factories	6	2	5	3	3	2	3	24
2.	Crushing capacity (TCD)	10250	3750	10000	5000	5000	4750	3750	42500
3.	Total cane requirement for 160 days (lakh metric tonnes)	16.40	6.00	16.00	8.00	8.00	7.60	6.00	68.00
4.	Present average cane yield (metric tonnes/hectares)	51.86	47.94	49.04	62.28	51.24	52.99	57.47	53.26
5.	Total cane area required (hectares)	31623	12515	32625	12845	15612	11342	10440	127002
6.	Area under rattan	12649	5006	13050	5138	6244	5736	4176	51999
7.	Area under plant cane (5-6) hectares	18974	7509	19576	7707	9368	8606	6264	78004
8.	Every year seed changing area (hectares)	6324	2503	6525	2569	3122	2868	2088	25999
9.	Requirement of area under								
	(a) Certified seeds (hectares)	632.4	250.3	625.5	256.9	312.2	286.8	208.00	2572.1
	(b) Foundation seed (hectares)	63.2	25.0	65.2	25.6	31.2	28.6	20.8	259.6

Source: The Role of Biotechnology in Sugarcane Productivity and Sustainability, XII Annual State Level Sugarcane Development Workshop, Vasantdada Sugar Institute, Pune, 18-19 August, 1995.

the crop. The disease and the pest free healthy seed is required to be planted for ensuring good yield. The farmers generally are unaware of importance of healthy seed and they plant the seed available from their old crop or from the neighbour's old crop. This results in breeding of pests and spread of diseases on the planted crop, resulting in poor yield. The cooperative sugar factories, take the responsibility of supply of improved quality and of high yielding variety. But these factories cannot meet the requirement of all the members. Generally the sugar factories grow the first stage seed on their own farms and it is distributed for multiplication to the members in their own area.

It is observed from the table 6 that the Marathwada region is at present having 24 factories. The total crushing capacity and the total cane requirement of these factories come to 42,500 TCD and 68.00 lakh metric tonnes respectively. In Marathwada region the present average per hectare cane yield is worked out to be 53.26 metric tonnes. The total area under cane required is worked out to be 1,27,002 hectares out of which the distribution comes to 51,999 hectares area under rattan and 78,004 hectares area under plant cane. From the total plant cane area about one-third (i.e. 25,999 hectares) area is required under the new planting in every year. Therefore, the requirement of certified and foundation seed area calculated to be 2,572.1 hectares and 259.6 hectares respectively.

From table 7 it could be observed that in Marathwada the major sugarcane varieties grown are Co740, Co7219, Co7527, Co8014, Coc671 and Co 86032. The compiled data from sugar factories indicated that in the Marathwada region Co740 occupied 22.79 per cent of total sugarcane area during 1997-98.

The data presented in table 7 indicates that the Co7219 is the most important new variety of sugarcane grown in Marathwada as it covered 44.95 per cent of the total area under sugarcane in the region during 1997-98. The next important variety of sugarcane grown in this region is Co

740. But the fact is that area under this variety of sugarcane is declining fasterly in recent times due to the discouragement to sugarcane growers from the sugar factory in this region. The sugar factories in this region are now recommending Co671 and Co 8014 along with Co 86032 varieties to sugarcane growers in recent times. So the area under these varieties in Marathwada has started increasing at a faster rate.

Table 7
Districtwise Varietal Performance Area in Marathwada in 1997-98

District	*Varietywise % area*							
	Co 740	*Co 7219*	*Co 7527*	*Co 8014*	*Co 671*	*Co 86032*	*Co 88121*	*Other*
Aurangabad	69.97	14.59	0.00	3.95	1.94	0.00	0.00	9.55
Jalna	19.01	54.69	0.15	14.65	5.73	1.08	0.86	3.83
Beed	33.81	34.86	2.15	23.65	2.81	0.71	0.00	2.01
Parbhani	4.20	74.41	0.00	5.58	3.93	0.00	0.00	11.88
Nanded	4.33	66.36	0.00	14.15	2.68	1.60	0.00	10.88
Osmanabad	9.50	55.70	0.42	6.40	21.50	0.41	0.00	8.12
Latur	18.76	14.08	0.00	4.31	53.92	0.00	0.00	8.88
Average	22.79	44.95	0.38	10.33	13.11	0.54	0.12	7.78
Marathwada	159.58	359.64	3.10	83.02	105.62	4.34	0.98	62.93

Source: Working Results of Sugar Factories in Maharashtra, Vasantdada Sugar Institute, Pune, 1997-98.

WELFARE MEASURES

In this area, achievement of Marathwada sugar cooperatives deserve to be written in golden letters. Following the footsteps of Pravara, Warna and Datta Shirole, almost all the sugar cooperatives in Marathwada have tried to excel in their social responsibility, by establishing primary and secondary schools, higher level educational colleges, professional institutions in engineering and medicine, hospitals, family welfare centres, consumer stores and housing facilities.

Educational Facilities

The Table 8 shows the data about educational facilities provided by sugar factories in Marathwada in 1998-99. It is seen from the table that out of 22 sugar factories, only factories in two districts i.e. Aurangabad and Latur have started pre-primary schools in their area of operation. Factories have started 18 primary schools and 20 sugar factories have provided the high school level educational facilities. It means almost all the sugar factories in Marathwada have tried to provide school level educational facilities in their area of operation . The sugar factories have realised the importance of education and tried to provide educational facilities through opening schools and colleges in their area of operation. Sugar factories in three districts havealso started English Schools mainly for the children of sugarcane growers. Sugar factories in Latur and Nanded districts have also started junior and senior colleges with Arts, Commerce and Science faculties. Some sugar factories have also started engineering colleges and ITIs in their area of operation. The sugarcane growers have been provided with the technical educational facilities by the sugar cooperatives in Marathwada. But none of the sugar factories in

Table 8
Educational Facilities Provided by the Sugar Factories in Marathwada in 1998-99

Sr. No.	*District*	*Pre-primary school*	*Primary school*	*High School*	*English Medium school*	*Higher Secondary School*	*College*
1.	Aurangabad	2	2	4	1	1	–
2.	Jalna	–	2	2	–	1	–
3.	Parbhani	–	3	3	–	–	–
4.	Beed	–	4	3	1	1	–
5.	Latur	1	2	3	–	1	1
6.	Nanded	–	3	2	1	1	1
7.	Osmanabad	–	2	2	–	1	1
	Marathwada	3	18	20	3	5	3

Source: Annual Reports of All Sugar Factories in Marathwada.

Marathwada has started any medical college for the children of the sugarcane growers.

Health and Credit Facilities

The Cooperative sugar factories in Marathwada have undertaken socio-economic activities like starting of health centre, cooperative credit society and consumer stores (see table 9). The sugar factories in all the districts have provided medical facilities at factory site through the health care centre. The medical facilities for first aid are supplied by the factory, free of cost to the employees.

Table 9
Health Centres, Cooperative Credit Societies and Consumer Stores Run by the Sugar Cooperatives in Marathwada in 1998-99.

Sr. No.	*District*	*Health centres*	*Cooperative Credit Societies*	*Consumer Stores*
1.	Aurangabad	5	2	–
2.	Jalna	2	–	–
3.	Parbhani	3	3	1
4.	Beed	4	2	–
5.	Latur	3	1	–
6.	Nanded	3	1	–
7.	Osmanabad	2	2	–
	Marathwada	22	12	1

Source: Annual Reports of All Sugar Factories in Marathwada.

Six sugar factories in Marathwada have started cooperative credit society for their employees. The cooperative credit society of the workers provides loan to needy workers and also the activity of supply of consumer articles at the reasonable cost is done by this society. These factories have provided rent free accommodation to the society. Sugar factories in Parbhani district have started consumer stores on cooperative basis. These factories have provided premises free of cost for the employees' cooperative consumer stores started at the factory site.

Housing Facilities

Generally, majority of sugar factories are located in rural area. The workers are from several villages or towns. So housing facilities must be provided by sugar factories to their workers. The housing facility may be provided free or on minor rent basis. It is the fact that all sugar factories have provided quarters to workers on minor rent basis but its quarters are temporarily constructed by factories. There are four categories of quarters viz. A, B, C and D. Sugar factories in Latur district (Manjara and Killari sugar factories) have provided good constructed quarters to their employees. It is exceptional case in Marathwada.

Employees' Provident Fund

In order to mitigate the hardship caused to the employees on retirement, the Employees' Provident Fund Act 1952 was passed. The act applies to the whole of India except the state of Jammu and Kashmir. It applies to all factories (in which at least 20 persons are employed) engaged in manufacturing sugar, cement, electrical, mechanical, engineering products etc. A more comprehensive provident fund scheme has been drawn up for workers employed in factories under the Employees' Provident Fund and Family Pension Fund Act, 1952. The period of service of a worker for eligibility to membership of the fund which was previously one year's continuous service or 240 days of actual work in a factory or in establishment has since been reduced to half with effect from 1st July 1974. The rate of contribution by employees as well as employer was 6¼ per cent of emoluments which has already been raised to 8 per cent in a number of industries including sugar industry. The scheme now applies to all sugar factory workers.

The object of the Act, as already seen, is to provide for the institution of the provident fund for employees in factories and other establishment. The principal duty is laid on the employer to put the provident fund scheme into operation and to make contribution of both their and employees share to the fund and to deduct from the wages of the employees their share. Now provident fund scheme applies to all sugar factories in Marathwada.

Family Pension Scheme

The employees' family pension scheme introduced from 1st March, 1971 affords regular income by way of pension to families of workers in case of their premature death. In case of a member who has contributed to the scheme for a period of not less than two years, the family pension scheme provides four kinds of benefits namely:

1. Family pension.
2. Life assurance.
3. As retirement benefit.
4. Withdrawal benefits.

The family pension scheme is applicable to all sugar factories but not followed by sugar factories yet.

The cooperative sugar factories in Marathwada have taken up many schemes of area development. The cooperative sugar factories can play vital role in starting these activities in the area by coordinating different agencies, for the benefit of the labourers in the area. The schemes and activities undertaken are also of very inadequate nature. There is a vast scope in the field of irrigation development by taking lift irrigation schemes, wherever possible bore wells, bandharas, construction of new wells and deepening of old one. In this area also, the sugar factory has to perform the role of catalyst, by promoting these activities and coordinating various agencies for the benefit of the area.

The cooperative sugar factories can do better in the field of rural development, if their primary objective of maximum capacity utilization with profitability is achieved. The factories may undertake the schemes of rural development on the basis of extensive survey of the area and after identifying the need of various activities.

Sugar factories have additional employment contributed to irrigation development. The sugarcane growers have been provided with the technical educational facilities by the sugar cooperatives in Marathwada. The cooperative sugar factories have undertaken socio-economic activities like starting of health centre, cooperative credit society and consumer stores at the factory site. All the sugar factories have provided medical facilities at factory site through the health centre. The medical facilities for first aid are supplied by the factory free of cost to the employees. All the sugar factories in Marathwada have provided quarters to workers on minor rent basis.

References

1. Venkatappaiah B., Report of the Steering Committee to Assess the Socio-Economic Impact of the Cooperative Sugar Factories, Council for Social Development, New Delhi, 1981.
2. Report on the Impact of Cooperative Sugar Factories on Rural Development, National Cooperative Development Corporation, New Delhi, 1982-83.
3. Inamdar N.R., Government and Cooperative Sugar Factories, Popular Prakashan, Bombay, 1965.
4. Circular No. DS/DEV-II/Cane Development, Officer of the Director of Sugar, Maharashtra State, Pune, 4th May, 1984.

7

Findings and Policy Measures

The sugar industry is the second largest agro-based industry in India next to textile. Though the New Guinea and its neighbouring islands in the South Pacific are now widely believed to be the natural home of sugarcane, the Indian sugar industry is one of the oldest industries in the country. In fact India is considered as the original home for sugar and sugarcane. About 327 B.C. when Alexander the great invaded India, he and his soldiers were the first European to see sugarcane in India. On their return home, they took sugarcane to Europe. However, it was about 700 A.D. that sugarcane was actually cultivated there. It was between the fourth and sixth century that the art of sugarcane making was discovered in India.

It is now an accomplished fact that the soil and climatic conditions of Maharashtra State are favourable for the plantation of sugarcane. The state is located in tropical belt. This belt is famous all over the world as it consists of most suitable area for raising sugarcane crop. Majority of the countries producing sugar are situated in this belt. On account of this geographically advantageous position, Maharashtra is renounced as 'sugar bowl' of the country.

The sugar industry is the second largest agro-based processing industry in India, having certain unique features of its own. It is a seasonal industry, based on a perishable raw material, viz. sugarcane with by-products like molasses, baggasse etc. It has a great significance which cannot be undervalued in its relation to agriculture and industrial economy of the rural regions of India. Fundamentally it affects agriculture. As such the expansion of sugar industry in India is an indispensable point for the upliftment of the socio-economic life of the rural masses, located in the rural areas, it has provided the most effective instrument for carrying progressive trends into the deeper country side.

The growth of sugar industry in India has helped the economy in many ways. The cooperative sugar factories have played pivotal role in modernisation of agriculture and in the socio-economical and educational transformation of rural society. Taking into account the importance of sugar industry in the national economy a number of researchers have worked on the various aspects of sugar industry such as the development and problems of the sugar industry and its prospects. Similarly, government policy and regional planning for sugar industry area, labour situation of the industry, impact of the industry on the lives of farmers and agriculture, the importance of sugar cooperatives in the rural economy and such other aspects of the industry also have been probed into.

Thus, various scholars have studied the different aspects of the sugar industry separately. It should bo omphasised here that whenever a particular factory is established in a region, it influences the economy of the region from all the angles. Hence, it would be better to take into consideration the impact of a factory as a whole and not by parts. In the present study, in addition to these aspects already mentioned, attempt has been made to study the growth of sugar cooperatives and its impact on economic development as a whole as influenced by the sugar factory in its area of operation.

The government policy regulates almost every aspect of sugar industry such as regulation and pricing of sugarcane, quality, storage and release of sugar stocks, control over price and distribution of by-products like molasses and alcohol, regulation of wages etc. Similarly financing of sugar industry, be it for financing of new projects of credit facilities for other purpose like purchase of cane, stock of sugar etc. is severely controlled by the financial institutions and banks under overall directions from Government of India or Reserve Bank of India. Even with regard to the sale of free quota sugar, its release, trading and stocking by the traders, the regulations are so severe that not much is left for the market speculation.

Sugarcane crop is grown in several rainfall, temperature and soil regions. However, sugarcane growing area could be grouped into sub-tropical and tropical belt. The states of Maharashtra, Gujarat, Andhra Pradesh, Tamil Nadu and Kerala comprise the 'tropical region' while the states of Punjab, Uttar Pradesh, Bihar and West Bengal comprise the 'sub-tropical' region.

The important sugarcane growing states of the tropical belt are Maharashtra, Karnataka, Andhra Pradesh, Tamil Nadu, Gujarat and Orissa. The temperature variation in the tropical belt is on an average 10°C to 12°C but it never drops to 5°C. Under these conditions the sugarcane growth and accumulation of sugar continue for longer period accounting for higher yield and recovery in these states. However, between these states located in the tropical belt yield recovery varies considerably due to difference in temperature, humidity, soil type, irrigation etc.

As per the state government norms, a sugar factory should have adequate supply of sugarcane at least for 160 days for 100 per cent capacity utilization in the Maharashtra State, and as per the national norms it must get adequate quantity of sugarcane for 180 days for 100 per cent capacity utilization. Generally, a crushing season starts during the third week of November and ends by the end of April.

The content of sugar in sugarcane crop is the result of agro-climatic factors and also other agronomic and cultural practices adopted in cultivation of sugarcane. The time of planting, variety planted, irrigation, manuring and fertilization of the crop, insect and disease control measures taken and the climatic and soil conditions are some of these factors related to the cultivation of sugarcane crop, which have the bearing on the sugar content. The other group of factors include the harvesting of the sugarcane at maturity stage and its transportation to the sugar factory without allowing the dry-age of the sugarcane before it is fed to the factory for crushing. The harvesting of sugarcane without leaving any stalk underground also proved to increase the sugar recovery.

The cooperative sugar factories, as the farmers organisations, have emerged as a leading force to give directions to the development of the rural areas. These factories did not remain only as the cooperative agro-processing units, but have become the centres of rural development. The cooperative sugar factories have provided employment to the large number of workers in the village country side. In the process of working of the sugar factories the effects on the growth of other ancillary industries and ancillary activities are also seen. The small and medium size industries producing the machinery parts, chemicals have developed in the area, likewise the industries based on the waste products of the sugar factories have been developed in some areas. Thus the backward and forward linkages in the process of economic development have been and are being established, because of the cooperative sugar factories.

The Maharashtra state government was initially interested in the success of these cooperative sugar factories because on it depended the validity of its policy of advancing the cooperative institutions as an alternative to either the private sector or the completely government owned public sector. It was vitally connected with the farmers. Its tenancy laws affected the farmers who were the producer member of the cooperative sugar factories. Apart from this the state government possessed the general authority to amend the matters in regard to the cooperative sugar factories.

The present study is undertaken mainly to study the policy of the central and state governments towards the sugar industry with particular reference to cooperative sugar factories. It aimed at to study the growth trends in area, production and yield of sugarcane in factory areas of Marathwada, the growth trends in sugarcane crushed, production of sugar, prices paid by cooperative sugar factories and recovery of sugar in Marathwada. The study also aimed at to study the impact of sugar cooperatives on employment, irrigation development, education and social life of people in Marathwada.

Marathwada, a backward region of Maharashtra State, has good potential for sugarcane cultivation and development of sugar industry. The land of Marathwada is very fertile and the climate is suitable for growing sugarcane crop. Sugar industry adds to the income of the farmers, provides casual and permanent employment, helps to earn foreign exchange and also helps to develop various kinds of ancillary and by-product industries. This leads to good industrial development and economic development of the region.

The present study pertained to Marathwada region and covered the period of 18 years from 1980-81 to 1997-98. At present there are 35 cooperative sugar factories operating in Marathwada, 22 sugar factories were operating in the year 1980-81. These sugar factories were considered for the present study.

FINDINGS

The main findings of the present study are summarised below:

1. Maharashtra is one of the leading sugarcane growing states in India. It is a perennial irrigated crop grown in all the zones of the state. Maharashtra state occupied a well recognized place of pride on the sugarcane map of the country. The area under sugarcane in the

Maharashtra state was 5.26 lakh hectares and have total sugar production of 351 lakh metric tonnes and yield 83.13 tonnes per hectare. There were 124 sugar factories working in Maharashtra in 2003-04, having on an average 100 per cent capacity utilization during the study period.

2. Overall average utilization of plant capacity in Maharashtra state was between 85.83 per cent and 99.36 per cent. In Marathwada, the production of sugarcane in factory areas was 68.90 lakh tonnes during 1996-97. Area under sugarcane was 105.1 thousand hectares and the yield of sugarcane was 84.2 tonnes per hectare during 1996-97.
3. The total number of crushing days of sugar factories in Marathwada have shown a decreasing trend during the period 1981-82 to 1986-87 from 228 days to merely 95 days. Thereafter, the number of crushing days has shown a mixed trend. For the entire period under study, the average number of crushing days amounts to about 167 days, which is higher than the required 160 days for full utilization of crushing capacity of sugar factories in Marathwada. It is also important to note that the number of crushing days was more than 200 days in five years. Further, during the years the crushing season of sugar factories exceeded 160 days. The district-wise picture reveals that the average number of crushing days for the whole period of twenty three years exceeded 160 days in case of all the districts in Marathwada except Parbhani district.
4. It is found that there has been continuous rising trend in price declared by state and central governments during 1981-82 to 1999-2000.
5. It is found that there have been huge fluctuations in cane crushed over the period in all the districts of Marathwada. If we consider the whole period, it is seen that the per year sugarcane crushed is found to be the highest in case of Aurangabad district (i.e. 9.98 lakh

metric tonnes) followed by Beed district (i.e. 6.97 lakh metric tonnes), Jalna district lies at the bottom in case of sugarcane crushed per year during the same period. The quantity of cane crushed per year in Parbhani, Nanded, Osmanabad and Latur districts was near about 5 lakh metric tonnes during the study period. The average annual growth rate of cane crushed was the highest in case of Aurangabad district i.e. 26.33 per cent due to more production of sugarcane and crushing capacity of factories and it was the lowest in case of Beed district i.e. 6.15 per cent per year during the period under consideration.

6. During 1981-82, sugar output in Marathwada was 36.74 lakh quintals, which increased and reached up to 56.01 lakh quintals in 1998-99. The sugar output in Marathwada was the highest of 71.62 lakh quintals in 1994-95 and the lowest of 16.07 lakh quintals in 1983-84. The sugar output in Marathwada is found to have grown at the annual rate of 16.35 per cent during the period under study. Among the seven districts the sugar factories of Aurangabad district have produced the highest sugar output followed by sugar factories in Latur and Beed districts. Jalna district lies at the bottom with respect to sugar production. Aurangabad district indicates highest growth in sugar output followed by Beed and Jalna districts in that order during the study period.

7. It is found that Aurangabad and Parbhani district show a very high recovery percentage (i.e. 10.19 and 10.18 per cent respectively) followed by Latur, Osmanabad, Beed, Nanded and at last Jalna district. Aurangabad, Parbhani and Latur districts have achieved a recovery level higher than 10 per cent during the study period and remaining four districts have enjoyed recovery percentage of sugar as Jalna 9.43 per cent, Beed 9.85 per cent, Nanded 9.68 per cent and Osmanabad 9.97 per cent during the period under study.

8. The study indicated that a sugar factory with 1250 tonnes daily crushing capacity has provided employment to 365 persons and seasonal employment to 343 persons. A sugar factory with 2500 tonnes daily crushing capacity has provided permanent employment to 461 persons and seasonal employment to 417 persons and a sugar factory with 3500 tonnes daily crushing capacity has provided permanent employment to 646 persons and seasonal employment to 653 persons. It is pointed out by some scholars that sugar cooperatives in Marathwada employ about ten to fifteen per cent workers more than requirements. The employment of surplus workers leads to increase in the cost of production which ultimately result in losses for the factories.
9. The sugar factories require 160 crushing days as per state norms to utilise its full capacity. But the sugar factories in Marathwada have experienced excess crushing days and more so during 1990-91 and 1995-96. This leads to generation of additional employment for seasonal and casual labourers. This study has indicated that the additional employment generated as per the state level norms was 89,10,550 days in 1990-91 and 71,85,900 days in 1995-96. The per factory additional employment generated is found to be 4,05,025 days in 1990-91 and 3,26,631 days in 1995-96.
10. The study indicated that in Aurangabad district, based on the information of three sugar factories, the total operational area of sugar factories was 4,32,094 hectares in 1995-96 and irrigated area was 1,07,722 hectares i.e. 24.93 per cent. The area irrigated by wells, canals, lift irrigation and K.T. weirs/bandharas was 86,635 hectares, 17,951 hectares, 2,353 hectares and 783 hectares respectively. The percentage to irrigated area by these sources comes to 80.42 per cent, 16.66 per cent, 2.18 per cent and 0.74 per cent respectively.
11. The sugar factories have realised the importance of education and tried to provide educational facilities

through opening schools and colleges in their area of operation. Few sugar factories have also started English schools mainly for the children of sugarcane growers. Many sugar factories have also started junior and senior colleges with arts, commerce and science faculties. Some sugar factories have also started engineering colleges and ITIs in their area of operation. The sugarcane growers have been provided with the technical education facilities by the sugar cooperatives in Marathwada. The cooperative sugar factories have undertaken socio-economic activities like starting the health centre, cooperative credit society and consumer stores at the factory site. All the sugar factories have provided medical facilities at factory site through the health care centre. The medical facilities for first aid are supplied by the factory free of cost to the employees.

POLICY MEASURES

1. The Government of India should consider to change the policy of licensing the new sugar factories at least for industrially backward areas and consider the proposals of new sugar factories from such areas based on the availability and potential for development of adequate sugarcane to feed the factory, instead of insisting on the availability of adequate standing sugarcane to meet the requirements of the new sugar factory before the sugar factory is established. This would be justified on the ground that adequate sugarcane to meet the requirement of the sugar factory would not be available in backward area otherwise the priority assigned to the proposals of sugar factories from backward area will have no meaning.
2. It is found that the crushing season of sugar factories in Marathwada is much below than the expectation. It is expected that the factory should have a crushing season of 180 days but actual crushing season varies very significantly. The variation is mainly on account of supply of sugarcane. The supply side of sugarcane is

determined by prevailing prices, government incentives and disincentives and factory's attitude towards their member cultivators. It appears that the absence of long term and stable government policy towards sugar marketing and sugarcane prices creates imbalances in demand and supply of sugarcane. Therefore, it is necessary to have stable defined policy matter.

3. The policy that no licence would be granted to the new sugar factory within a radius of 40 kms of the existing unit may be strictly adhered to, to avoid the overlapping of the areas resulting in many problems in the working of the sugar factories concerned.
4. It is recommended that sugar factories should take effective, concrete and continuous programme of sugarcane development. The factory should have separate department for sugarcane development and for sugarcane supply the sugarcane development departments should be adequately staffed with the experts in the field of agronomy, soil science and plant pathology i.e. seed production and distribution of improved varieties, seed treatment etc. Some factories in Marathwada do not have such staff for sugarcane development. Hence there is need of appointing such staff by these factories.
5. The sugar factory should prepare a programme of sugarcane development and wherever necessary coordinate various agencies in furtherance of the programme. The yield per hectare in Marathwada is very low particularly due to very late planting coupled with poor agricultural technology adopted. It is necessary to plan the planting of the sugarcane in the area of operation of the factory from October to January so as to increase per hectare yield. The other practices like use of better and quality disease and pest free seed, seed treatment, timely and proper manuring and fertilisation, proper irrigation and pest and disease control will improve the yield of sugarcane substantially. It is

recommended that the planting of sugarcane in the area to be planted should be so planned that the adequate quantity of fully matured sugarcane would be available throughout the crushing season of the factory. The longest crushing season without affecting the recovery per cent adversely should be achieved. It is recommended that crushing season of the factories in Marathwada should start in the middle of October and should end in the middle of April. This will give the longest possible crushing season without affecting the recovery percentage adversely. Attempt should be made to increase sugarcane yield by 20 tonnes per hectare which is possible to overcome the scarcity of sugarcane.

6. The cooperative sugar factories in Marathwada should undertake more lift irrigation schemes with the help of various financial agencies. The promotional role in organising the lift can be played by the sugar factories. This will result in increase in area under sugarcane. The other schemes of irrigation development like bore wells, dug wells, bandharas should be promoted by the sugar factories with the help of different agencies.
7. From the study it is observed that many sugar cooperatives from Marathwada region do not utilise the loan facility provided by Sugar Development Fund (SDF) and Cane Development Fund (CDF) of the central and state government because of their ignorance. Therefore, every sugar factory must become conscious in exploiting the facilities provided by the government for the socio-economic development in the factory areas.

Bibliography

BOOKS

1. Agrawal R.N., *Sugar Industry of India, My Recollection,* Popular Prakashan Pvt. Ltd., Bombay, 1976.
2. Bapat N.G., *Economic Development of Ahmednagar District 1981-1960,* Bombay Progressive Corporation Pvt. Ltd., 1973.
3. Beachey R.W., *The British West Indies Sugar Industry in the late 19th Century,* Oxford Basil Blackwell, 1957.
4. Brahme Sulabha, Pore, Kumud and Pore S.H., *Regional Planning : A Case Study of Marathwada Region,* Gokhale Institute of Politics and Economics, Pune, 1975.
5. Caribbean Commission, *The Sugar Industry of the Caribbean Research Council, Washington,* 1947.
6. Chandra Satish, *Agricultural Price Policy in India,* Chug Publications, Allahabad, 1985.
7. Deer Noel, *History of Sugar,* Vol. I, Chapman and Hall Ltd., London, 1949.
8. Deshmukh Datta, Maharashtratil Sakhar Kampanya, *Mothya Usmalyvaril Kamgar Va Khandkari Zamin Malakancha Prashna,* Published by Datta Deshmukh, Sangamner, 1969.
9. Gadgil D.R., *Towards Cooperative Commonwealth,* Punjab University Publication Bureau, Chandigarh, 1961.
10. Gandhi M.G., *The Indian Sugar Industry, Its Present and Future,* Printed and Published by Mrs. J.N. Ghosh at the Star Printing Works, Calcutta, 1934.

11. Gadgil D.R., *Sugar Cooperatives in Maharashtra,* Published by the National Federation of Cooperative Sugar Factories Ltd., New Delhi, 1961.
12. Government of Maharashtra, Department of Agriculture and Cooperation, *Integrated Area Development Scheme for Small Farmers and Agriculture Labour* (Supplementary Pamphlet Containing Important Government Orders), Bombay, 1971.
13. Inamdar N.R., *Government and Cooperative Sugar Factories,* Popular Prakashan, Bombay, 1965.
14. *Indian Sugar Supplement,* Indian Sugar Syndicate Ltd., Kanpur, 1948.
15. Jain A.P., *Foreword to Growers Own Cooperative Sugar Factories,* Ministry of Food and Agriculture, Government of India, New Delhi, 1956.
16. Johnson, G.D. *The Sugar Programme : Large Costs and Small Benefits,* American Enterprise Institute for Public Policy Research, Washington, 1974.
17. Kharche R.M., *Sugar Cooperatives in Developed Economy,* Parimal Prakashan, Aurangabad, 1989.
18. Kharkar N.C., *Maharashtratil Sakhar Karkhanyache Mulyamapan Parisamwad,* Published by the Registrar, Deccan Sugar Technologists Association, Pune, 1976.
19. Kulkarni D.G., *Tropical Sugar,* Dhyanjoti Prakashan, Pune, 1971.
20. Maharashtra State Cooperative Land Development Bank Ltd., Bombay, *Manual of Loaning,* 1976.
21. Malyadri V., *Socio-Economic Impact of the Sugar Cooperatives,* Commerce Prakashan, Bombay, 1975.
22. Mohite Y.J., *Sugarcane Industry of Maharashtra* (A Blue Print for Progress), Government of Maharashtra, Bombay, 1974.
23. Nankar J.T., *Scope and Prospects of Intercropping of Potato in Sugarcane in Maharashtra,* 34th Convention, Deccan Sugar Technologists Association, Pune, 1984.
24. National Federation of Cooperative Sugar Factories Ltd., *Cooperative Sugar Directory and Year Book,* New Delhi, 1984.
25. Paturau J. Maurice, *By-products of the Cane Sugar Industry,* Elsevier Publishing Company, Amsterdam, London, 1969.
26. Ram Vichar Sinha, N., *Sugar Industry in India,* Deep and Deep Publications, New Delhi, 1968.

27. Sadhu A.N. and Mahajan R.K., *Technological Change and Agricultural Development in India,* Himalaya Publishing House, New Delhi, 1985.

28. Srivastav U.K., George R.S. and Sharma S.L., *Rural Development Project Through Voluntary Agency,* Indian Institute of Management, Ahmedabad, 1975.

29. Singhal Vikas, *Handbook of Indian Agriculture,* Vikas Publishing House Private Limited, New Delhi, 1995.

30. Tacke E.F., *The World Sugar Economy: Structure and Policies,* Vol. II, Published by International Sugar Council in 1963.

31. Virioto Gutierrez, *World Sugar Problem 1929-35,* Normal Rodger 2, St. Dunstan's Hill, E.C. 3, London, 1935.

32. Vladimir P., Timoshenko and Boris C. Swerling, *The World Sugar,* Stanford University Press, California, 1975.

JOURNALS AND PERIODICALS

1. Anand D.P., Finance and Accounting for the Sugar Industry, *Indian Sugar,* 1975.

2. Anonymous, Company Affairs, Eid-Parry (India) Ltd., *Indian Sugar,* 1979.

3. Auty R.M., Some Problems in Identifying Scale Economies in the Sugar Industry of Danerab, *World Economics and Rural Sociology Abstract,* 1973.

4. Chekkapan, *Socio Economic Impact of Sugar Cooperatives,* Financial Express, 1976.

5. The Institute of Cost and Work Accountants of India, *Cost Audit in Sugar Industry,* Cost Accountant's Hall, 12, Sudder Street, Calcutta, 1971.

6. Dinesh C., Income Distribution Through Sugar Cooperatives, *The Economic Times,* 4 August, 1976.

7. *Economic Trends,* Vol. XIII, June 16, 1984, Published by Y.L. Sood for FICCI, Federation House, Tansen Marg, New Delhi.

8. *Economic Trends,* Vol. XIII, Sept. 16, 1985, Published by Y.L. Sood for FICCI, Federation House, Tansen Marg, New Delhi.

9. Ferron Oliva D.P., Sugar Industry in Bihar Diagnosis and Remedy, *Indian Sugar,* 1976.

10. Fuss F.W., Cooperative Factories in India, *World Agricultural Economics and Rural Sociology Abstract,* 1968.

11. Gustab Mikusah, *Sugar: Encyclopaedia of the Social Sciences,* Vol. XIV, The Macmillan Co., New York, 1963.
12. Hapse D.G., Sugar Development Technology for Maharashtra, *Maharashtra Sugar,* 1982.
13. Hinge V.N., Pawar J.R. and Narwadkar D.S., Production Performance of Cooperative Sugar Units in Maharashtra, *Indian Journal of Agricultural Economics,* XIV(3), 1989.
14. Hirunandas J., Denabox F. and Corina M., Study on Economics of Scale in Raw Sugar Factories, *The International Sugar Journal,* July, 1971.
15. Indian Sugar Mills Association, *Indian Sugar Supplement,* Sugar House, 39 Nehru Palace, New Delhi, 1948.
16. The Indian Sugar Mills Association, *Indian Sugar Year Book,* Vol. I, New Delhi, 1983-84.
17. Ingram L., Fuel and Chemical Feed Stock from Sugarcane in Central America, *International Sugar,* 1980.
18. Kamat G.S., Management of Cooperative Sugar Factories in Maharashtra, *The Maharashtra Cooperative Quarterly,* LIX (3), 1975.
19. Kamat G.S., Socio Economic Impact of Sugar Cooperative on Rural Area, *Cooperative Sugar,* August, 1972.
20. Kaul J.L., A Study of Supply Response to Price of Punjab Crops, *Indian Journal of Agricultural Economics,* Vol. V, 1967.
21. Kharche R.M., Cooperative Sugar Factories and Industrial Growth of Marathwada, *Maharashtra Cooperative Quarterly,* Vol. II, April 1976.
22. Kharkar N.C., Technological Evaluation of Sugar Factories in Maharashtra, *Deccan Sugar Technologists Association,* Pune, 1975.
23. Kirilyak A.P. and Kirilyak L.A., The Production Capacity of Sugar Factory and Optimum Campaign Length, *International Sugar Journal,* February, 1971.
24. Kuchhadiya D.B., Shiyani B.L. and Parmar G.D., An Economic Analysis of Sugarcane Crop, *Indian Sugar,* 1988.
25. Manohar Rao P., By-products Utilization in Sugar Industry, *Maharashtra Sugar,* 1980.
26. Manohar Rao P., Development of Indian Sugar Industry – Historical, *Bharatiya Sugar Directory,* 1987.

27. Mehta J.S., Sugar Production Reaches New Peak under Partial-Decontrol, *Supplement to Capital,* 1969.

28. Mittal B.L., Rehabilitation and Modernization of Sugar Factories, Sugar Technology, *Indian Sugar,* 1976.

29. Mujumdar N.A., Crop Pattern, Production Target and Strategic Intervention, *Indian Journal of Agricultural Economics,* Vol. VI, 1963.

30. Murali P., Sugar Industry Planning and Controlling Profiles, *Maharashtra Sugar,* 1980.

31. Patil M.K., Rehabilitation and Modernization of Cooperative Sugar Industry, *Maharashtra Sugar,* 1976.

32. Pawar G.R. and Kshirsagar S.M., Growth Rate in Area, Production and Productivity of Sugarcane in Comparison with Important Cash Crop in Maharashtra, *Maharashtra Sugar,* 1979.

33. Puranik A.D., Cooperative Sugar Factory as an Instrument of Economic Development, *Maharashtra Sugar,* Vol. I, December 1975.

34. Puranik A.D., A Case Study of the Problems of Economic Development in the Area of Operation of Cooperative Sugar Factory, *Maharashtra Sugar,* June 1976.

35. Puranik A.D., Special Article on the Burning Problems of Cooperative Sugar Factories and Water, *Maharashtra Sugar,* Vol. I, March, 1976.

36. Puranik A.D., Sugar Cooperative – a Case Against Nationalization, *Cooperative Information Bulletin,* July, 1972.

37. Raghwaih and Singh P.P., Yield and Nitrogen Uptake of Sugarcane Varieties at Graded Level of Nitrogen, *Indian Sugar,* 1980.

38. Raghwendra P.G., Sugar Factories and Their Problems, *Maharashtra Sugar,* 1977.

39. Ramesh N.A., Adjudication of the Performance of Sugar Factories, *Maharashtra Sugar,* 1980.

40. Sakhalkar S.B., "Sugar Industry in Maharashtra", *Eastern Economist Maharashtra Supplement,* January, 1971.

41. Shah H.P. and Shah N.K., Measures for Reduction in Cost of Production of Sugar, *Gujarat Association for Agricultural Science,* 1980.

42. Sharma S.C., The Role of Sugar Industry in Rural Development with Special Reference to East Uttar Pradesh, North Bihar, *Indian Sugar,* 1981.

43. Shewade P.K., Some Points to Improve the Efficiencies of New Sugar Factories in Vidarbha, *Bharatiya Sugar,* 1989.

44. Singh K.V., Malik, Sanjeev Kumar and Lal Jagdish, Inter-regional Trend Analysis of Sugarcane Acreage, Production and Productivity in Uttar Pradesh, *Agricultural Situation in India,* Vol. XLIX, No. 3, May, 1994.

45. Singh L.N. and Singh K.M., A Study on Acreage Response to Price and Non-Price Determinants for Sugarcane in Bihar, *Indian Sugar,* January, 1993.

46. Singh Rajendra and Swaroop, Regional Differences in Sugarcane Output Growth in India, *Indian Sugar,* 1978.

47. Subbarao K., Farm Supply Response : A Case Study of Sugarcane in Andhra Pradesh, *Indian Journal of Agricultural Economics,* Vol. VII, 1969.

48. Thakare R.P., Veerkar P.D. and Joshi R.M., Regional Trends in Area, Production and Productivity of Sugarcane and Acreage Response in Maharashtra State, *Maharashtra Journal of Agricultural Economics,* Vol. VII, No. 1, March, 1995.

49. Waghmare P.R. and K.D. Rajmane, A Study of Change in Area, Production and Productivity Risk of Various Crops in Maharashtra and Different Districts of Marathwada, *Agrosco Report,* Department of Agricultural Economics and Statistics, Marathwada Agricultural University, Parbhani, 1979.

THESES

1. Andhale G.B., *A Study of the Impact of a Cooperative Sugar Factory on the Lives of Farmers,* M.Sc. (Agri.) Thesis, Mahatma Phule Krishi Vidyapeeth, Rahuri, 1972.

2. Jain N.S., *Regional Economic Planning in a Sugar Factory Area,* Ph.D. Thesis, University of Poona, 1976.

3. Kamat G.S., *Management of a Cooperative Enterprise with Special Reference to Sugar Cooperatives in Maharashtra,* Ph.D. Thesis, Poona University, 1965.

4. Kawade A.V., *Economics of Size and Returns to Scale in Cooperative Sugar Factories in Maharashtra,* M.Sc. (Agri.) Thesis, Mahatma Phule Agricultural University, Rahuri, 1977.

5. Patel K.S., *Economic Efficiency of Sugar Industry in Marathwada Region of Maharashtra State,* Unpublished Ph.D. Thesis, Submitted to Marathwada Agricultural University, Parbhani, June, 1991.
6. Pendse B.P., *Large-Scale Industries of Maharashtra,* M.A. Thesis, University of Bombay, 1950.
7. Raghavachari, V., *State and the Indian Sugar Industry,* Ph.D. Thesis, University of Poona, 1973.
8. Shirodkar S.L., *Cooperative Movement in Kolhapur District,* Ph.D. Thesis, University of Poona, 1967.
9. Tupe S.D., *The Impact of Sugar Factories on the Rural Economy – A Case Study,* Ph.D. Thesis, University of Poona, 1980.

REPORTS

1. Annual Reports of All Sugar Factories in Marathwada, 1981-82 to 1998-99.
2. Annual Reports of National Federation of Cooperative Sugar Factories Ltd., New Delhi, 1983.
3. Chief Statistician : Commissionerate of Agriculture, Pune, The Districtwise Area, Production and Productivity of Principal Crops in Maharashtra State, 1994-95 to 1995-96.
4. Deputy Director : Bureau of Economics and Statistics, Aurangabad Division, Aurangabad : Marathwada at a Glance, 1992-93.
5. Annual Reports of Maharashtra Rajya Sahakari Sakhar Karkhana Sangh Ltd., 1976-77 to 1995-96.
6. Annual Reports of Maharashtra Rajya Sahakari Sakhar Karkhana Sangh Ltd., Regional Office, Aurangabad, 1999-2000.
7. Government of India, Planning Commission, First Five Year Plan, New Delhi, 1950-55.
8. Government of India, Planning Commission, Third Five Year Plan, New Delhi, 1961-66.
9. Government of India, Planning Commission, Sixth Five Year Plan, New Delhi, 1980-85.
10. Government of Maharashtra, Agriculture and Cooperative Department, Epitome of Agriculture in Maharashtra, Part I and II, 1974-75 to 1995-96.

11. Report of Sugar Enquiry Commission, Government of India, 1965.
12. Report of the Committee of Exports for Making Recommendations for Formation of Zones the drawl of sugarcane by Sugar Factories in Maharashtra, Bombay, 1983.
13. Report of the Sugar Enquiry Commission, October 1965.
14. Report of the Agricultural Price Commission on Price Policy for Sugarcane, 1968-69.
15. Working Results of Sugar Factories in Maharashtra, 1981-82 to 1998-99, Vasantdada Sugar Institute, Pune.